2nd Edition

Dialectical Behavior Therapy

Volume I

The Clinician's Guidebook
for Acquiring
Competency in DBT

Cathy Moonshine, PhD, MAC, CADC-III
Stephanie Schaefer, PsyD, CADC-I

Published by
PESI Publishing & Media
PESI, Inc.
3839 White Ave
Eau Claire, WI 54703

Cover Design: Amy Rubenzer
Layout: Bookmasters & Amy Rubenzer

Proudly printed in the United States of America

ISBN: 9781683731894

Cathy Moonshine, PhD, MAC, CADC III and Stephanie Schaefer, PsyD, CADC I are not affiliated or associated with Marsha M. Linehan, PhD, ABPP, or her organizations.

PESI
Publishing
& Media
pesipublishing.com

Table of Contents

Chapter 1

Chapter 2

Clinical Presentations 107

Chapter 6

About the Authors

Dr. Cathy Moonshine has trained thousands of individuals nationally and internationally with creative methods and flexible thinking to show there is more than one way to successfully implement DBT. She has over 30 years of experience in public, university and private mental health and addictions treatment settings across all levels of care, serving as a clinician, supervisor and director.

Dr. Moonshine is the Behavioral Health Director at Hawaii Island Family Medicine Residency and Health Clinic at Hilo Medical Center on the Big Island of Hawaii. She is a professor emeritus at Pacific University in Oregon.

Dr. Stephanie Schaefer is a licensed psychologist, certified alcohol drug counselor (CADC I) in Portland, Oregon. She has worked with clients from a variety of backgrounds and in various settings, including both outpatient and residential community mental health settings. In addition, Dr. Schaefer has provided DBT and co-occurring disorders trainings regionally, nationally and internationally, and mentors colleagues and supervises graduate-level practicum students. Dr. Schaefer is a faculty counselor at Clackamas Community College, where she has the opportunity to teach and utilize DBT skills regularly.

Introduction

We wrote this book because we use Dialectical Behavior Therapy (DBT) in more flexible and creative ways than it was originally designed. We are not comprehensively trained DBT clinicians. We find that not having mandates about when and how to deliver DBT has freed us to explore the model and figure out how to customize it to our philosophy, values, and the characteristics and desires of the clients we work with. Having this flexible mindset has empowered us to successfully modify DBT to the demands and limitations of the settings we work in.

We have been both criticized and admired for using DBT in ways not originally designed or sanctioned. We accept this dialectic. We see strengths in our DBT frame while acknowledging we have drifted from the original model. Our adaptations are thoughtful and intentional. We always keep in mind the best interest of clients and refer certain clients to full-fidelity DBT programs when indicated. This typically happens when clients are chronically suicidal and need the intensity and after-hours access of a full-fidelity DBT program.

OUR JOURNEY

Our knowledge of DBT began in graduate school, both in classes and at practicum sites. We learned the full DBT model, the supporting research, and focused on adherence to the model. From there, we gained clinical experience, received clinical supervision, engaged in consultation, read many books and articles, and attended continuing education courses to increase our knowledge and application of DBT. While the full-fidelity model of DBT includes aspects that are very helpful for many clients with Borderline Personality Disorder (BPD), they didn't always fit well with the settings and populations we were working with. Eventually, we came to the conclusion that we could use DBT more flexibly to meet the needs of our clients.

As part of our journey, we have provided trainings to thousands of mental health professionals around the world, consulted with hundreds of treatment organizations about implementing and sustaining DBT, and supervised and consulted with countless mental health, addictions and medical professionals delivering DBT to clients. We have familiarity with nearly every level of care, including state hospitals, correctional institutions, community mental health centers, Veteran's Administration, school systems and private practices. Additionally, we have learned from other professionals, clients and their family members, and stakeholders, which has informed our DBT practices; and we have integrated components from other worthwhile models—such as Motivational Interviewing—into our use of DBT. We have found doing all of these from a trauma-informed framework is essential.

ADAPTING DBT

Through this process, we have refined our approach to delivering DBT in various settings and with different types of clients. This book is designed to help you make adjustments to make DBT fit, while still maintaining the integrity of DBT. Our focus is on maintaining a dialectical balance, being mindfully present, and making use of DBT skills. We have sought to employ the most successful aspects of the traditional DBT model in combination with our own triumphs and lessons learned as clinicians and supervisors—perhaps the most important lessons coming from our own missteps, miscalculations, and mistakes, and what our clients have taught us about tenacity, resiliency and grace.

We believe being fallible and learning from mistakes is consistent with DBT. These aspects empower clinicians and clients to do the best they can in life while learning how to deal with challenges and crises in effective ways.

For the majority of clients we have treated and the different settings we have worked in, formal DBT wasn't feasible or practical. We want to share our ideas and clinical experience with other clinicians and program administrators to provide options for modifying and adjusting DBT in their practices. These are just ideas. Some of them will probably resonate with you while others will not. You may find that our ideas and examples are a starting point for you to create your own unique way of applying DBT.

You might want to use DBT:

- in creative and flexible ways: You can!

- with a variety of presenting problems and diagnoses: No problem!

- with other orientations and interventions: Absolutely!

- in nontraditional settings and formats: Go for it!

There are many clients who benefit from full-fidelity DBT; and there are also many, many clients who benefit from DBT practiced more creatively and flexibly. This text provides ideas, strategies, and examples of ways to integrate DBT into your practice—whether a private practice, community mental health center, addictions treatment program, intensive outpatient/partial hospitalization program, residential program, inpatient hospital, or primary care office.

Not only can DBT be used to treat individuals with mental health and substance use disorders, but it can also be used as a resiliency program to foster healthy development and functioning. This text explores:

1. The framework and function of the full-fidelity practice of DBT.

2. Integrating the philosophy, techniques, and strategies of DBT into clinical practice to create an effective, customized DBT clinical process.

3. The importance of being dialectical for both the clients and the clinicians.

4. How the Meta Skills, Secondary Skills, and Ancillary Skills will increase client functioning and life satisfaction.

5. A variety of options for using DBT with a wide assortment of clinical presentations, including clients with mental health issues, addictions problems, and dual diagnoses.

6. Utilizing DBT in a variety of settings, formats, and across the lifespan.

7. Including diversity along every step of the way in DBT with clients.

8. How DBT will improve clinician self-care and build resiliency in our clinical practices.

WITH GRATITUDE

More than three generations of mental health clinicians, and tens of thousands of individuals along with their families are grateful to Dr. Marsha Linehan and her colleagues who created, researched, delivered and disseminated DBT over the last 25 years. This model has saved lives; it has contributed to improved relationships and family functioning all while saving money and mental health resources. Garnering such widespread attention may not have been Dr. Linehan's goal, and yet DBT has significantly changed mental health treatment, the diagnostic manual, and our communities.

We are grateful that DBT changed the course of our careers and helped so many of the clients we have worked with. In addition, we are grateful to have had opportunities to share our knowledge and experience with DBT in graduate courses, continuing education trainings, clinical supervision, professional consultation and our writings. We look forward to hearing how you adapt DBT to fit with your settings, theoretical orientations, and client populations in the next 25 years.

Chapter 1

The DBT Model:
Adaptations and Modifications

HOW IT ALL BEGAN

2018 marked the 25th anniversary since Dr. Marsha Linehan published *Cognitive-Behavioral Treatment of Borderline Personality Disorder* and *Skills Training Manual for Treating Borderline Personality* (Linehan, 1993a; Linehan, 1993b). Although there were a number of peer-reviewed articles published in professional journals prior to this date, this was the first widespread text and skills manual for Dialectical Behavior Therapy (DBT). Since then, DBT has gained the interest of researchers, clinicians and clients. Today, there are over 1,000 articles and dozens of books that have been published on this topic (see PsycINFO). The popularity of DBT can be attributed to its demonstrated success with high-need, challenging clients.

DBT was originally created by Dr. Linehan to address the needs of chronically suicidal clients for whom the models in use at the time were insufficient (Linehan 1993a; Linehan 1993b). In many communities, there were dozens—perhaps hundreds—of chronically suicidal clients over-utilizing acute care resources such as emergency rooms and inpatient hospital beds. No matter what therapy some of these clients received or psychiatric medications they took, their lives were filled with self-hatred and despair.

Although families and other support networks engaged in various strategies to assist their loved ones, treatment professionals were at a loss as to how to adequately treat these clients in a manner that allowed them to live independently and with some degree of life satisfaction. Many professionals dedicated themselves to finding clinical methods or biological interventions that would meet these clients' needs.

For some clients, this resulted in relief of symptoms, remission, and perhaps even recovery from their mental health and substance use difficulties. However, for many clients, it felt like one failure after another. If their therapists, psychologists, psychiatric nurse practitioners, psychiatrists, and medical doctors couldn't collaborate with their friends and families to find an effective treatment, then the client felt hopeless and believed life wasn't worth living.

Treatment professionals from various backgrounds also believed it might be hopeless. Self-doubt and fears of incompetence plagued many professionals. Some professionals chose not to work with these clients, and in the worst-case scenarios, professionals acted out their own countertransference and negative emotional reactions by firing clients, becoming angry or immobilized, withdrawing, and finding other ways of disengaging from these clients.

Then along came DBT. Research revealed many of these chronically suicidal clients qualified for a diagnosis of Borderline Personality Disorder (BPD). Over the last three decades, many research studies have supported the efficacy of DBT in treating individuals with BPD, and more recently, effectiveness with other clinical presentations as well (Linehan, 2015).

There have been many modifications and adaptations of DBT since its inception. Some of these modifications have research support behind them and have gotten Dr. Linehan's approval. However, many modifications and adaptations have happened organically in various clinical settings or in individuals' lives. A plethora of DBT skills have been created by clinicians, some of whom have been intensively trained and many who have not. Other skills have been created by professors, teachers, mentors, and others. But perhaps the most powerful skills have been developed by clients, family members and support people.

While many of these adaptations and modifications haven't been tested in the research literature, there is anecdotal evidence from clients, their families, and treating clinicians that the modifications and adaptations are useful. For some, staying with the research-supported strategies of DBT makes the most sense, while others like to make things their own and enjoy the creativity allowed when one is not restricted to a research model—and there is value in both of these perspectives. Even Dr. Linehan built upon existing models in her development of DBT. She used existing psychological models, Buddhist teachings and well-established clinical thinking to help shape what we now know as DBT.

THEORY, PHILOSOPHY AND MAJOR GOAL

While the DBT model started as a manualized Cognitive Behavioral Therapy (CBT), it has become a therapeutic modality that is used worldwide with a variety of clinical presentations. The ultimate goal of DBT is to help individuals "build a life worth living," which can aid in decreasing destructive behavior, self-harm, and clinical symptoms, while also improving relationships and increasing level of functioning and life satisfaction. In addition, DBT is a therapeutic approach that is compatible with various other therapeutic modalities—such as CBT—and many integrated clinicians have added DBT's framework and tools to their repertoire.

Internal Experiences

DBT is based on the theory that clients with BPD have internal distress (Linehan, 2015). These clients are emotionally intuitive and sensitive and, as a survival mechanism, many clients have learned to pick up on how others feel about them. While their perceptions can be inaccurate, they are close enough to reality for these clients to engage in behavior based on how they think people feel about them. Clients use this ability to manage their relationships and behaviors. Often this BPD behavior is viewed as an attempt to control others, and this is when accusations of being manipulative occur against the client. Sometimes clients with BPD also accuse others of being manipulative.

Regardless of whether either party is intending to manipulate the other—which is a possibility—this is unhelpful and is a particularly important issue in the therapeutic relationship. It is essential that clinicians are aware of such behavior and are able to form genuine, empathic relationships with appropriate boundaries. Because clients will sense how their clinicians feel about them, it is particularly important for clinicians to maintain this "both/and" dialectical balance—both issues are important: the empathic relationships and the boundaries.

Being emotionally intense and slow to return to baseline are two internal experiences common to many clients experiencing BPD. These clients feel their emotions more intensely than the average person, whether those feelings are positive or negative. Instead of rating an emotion on a scale from 1 to 10, these clients' emotions are frequently rated as "off the chart." A 1 to 10 scale doesn't give them enough range because their experience is often an 11, 15 or 100. Additionally, these same clients may feel their emotions for an extended amount of time. For example, if it took an average person without BPD 30 to 45 minutes to return to baseline from a given emotional state, it might take these clients hours, days, or as much as a week to return to their baseline emotional state.

Because clients with BPD have more intense, chaotic, and troublesome internal experiences, they benefit from the here-and-now perspective, frustration tolerance, emotion regulation, and effectiveness in relationships skills provided by adopting a DBT perspective and using these skills in their lives.

External Experiences

If the client's internal experience is as described previously, it is not surprising that individuals with BPD may also have different experiences in their relationships and environments than the average person. According to DBT theory, these individuals hear from family, friends and authority figures that the ways they think, communicate, and behave are inappropriate, unacceptable and wrong; and they must think, communicate and behave in different ways. This is invalidating. These individuals are told to be completely different from their true selves, which is highly unlikely—if not impossible.

Another frequent experience is punishment or abuse when an individual displays painful emotions and problematic behaviors. Both children and adults sometimes act out their emotional experiences. For example, when they lose control of their tempers or become inconsolably sad, they may behave in problematic ways such as getting into physical fights, harming themselves, drinking alcohol, using drugs, engaging in out-of-control eating or in risky sexual encounters, gambling or spending excessively—among others. They reject help and don't think anything can help them manage their emotions more effectively. In fact, there may even be an attitude of self-righteousness or hopelessness in their defense of their emotions or behaviors. As a result, their emotions and behaviors can result in punishment or abuse from others who label them as excessive and over-the-top.

Additionally, these clients hear from their family and friends that their problems are not that bad and that they could find solutions a lot more easily if they just tried. Phrases such as: "Just get over it," "Stop making it worse than it needs to be," "Why aren't you more like _____," "You need to be less like _____" and "Stop being so dramatic" are just some of the things that these clients hear.

The Cumulative Effect of Internal and External Experiences

Because clients with BPD are characterized by the internal and external experiences mentioned, it makes sense that they are who they are. If these things happened once or twice, it probably wouldn't result in their current problems; but these chronic and entrenched experiences disrupt typical development. They have experienced disrespect, disappointment, and trauma again, and again and again. They have also been unable to access their skills, strengths and resilience effectively.

Given the skills-based nature of DBT—which allows clients to practice skills to fit differing situations—and the focus of the skills on four core areas clients with BPD struggle with, it is logical that these clients will benefit from DBT. This modality can provide the essential building blocks to rebuild their lives into lives worth living.

Reality is Subjective

Everyone experiences reality differently. Sometimes there are significant similarities in individuals' experiences of the same event, conversation or email; other times, there are very different experiences. Acknowledging that reality is subjective for every individual is a way in which individuals can agree to disagree. Each person's experience is real for them. We all distort things, fail to pay attention to certain details, pay greater attention to other details and interpret things in particular ways. Individuals bring their internal experiences, values, opinions, styles, moods and historical context to the present moment.

Words can also have multiple meanings. Tone of voice and nonverbal communication can be interpreted in a variety of ways. All of this impacts how individuals interpret and view their life events and day-to-day happenings. The biosocial theory tells us that clients—whether BPD clients, or those struggling with addictions, trauma or other personality disorders—are highly emotionally dysregulated, which has a large impact on how these individuals experience their world.

An important point to recognize is that invalidation is in the eyes of the beholder. What one person feels is invalidating may not be so to another person; so individuals may be thought of, or accused of, exaggerating or lying about their experience. However, from the DBT framework, each person's experience is valid and real for them. As clinicians, we want to understand what the client is expressing when they talk about experiences that are very different from ours or seem far-fetched. Is the client saying that they are hurt, disrespected, or feel unsafe? Even if we wouldn't have interpreted the cues in the same way as the client, we must remain respectful of their individual experience and interpretation.

PHILOSOPHICAL FOUNDATIONS

Clients are doing the best they can, and they would benefit from being more skillful and effective in their lives

Because these clients are highly sensitive, emotionally intense, slow to return to baseline, and find themselves living in invalidating environments with people who take advantage of, abuse and punish them, it only makes sense that they would engage in problematic and destructive behaviors. These clients are doing the best they can with what they've got. Working from a DBT framework provides compassion and understanding for these clients. This is a useful stance for both the clinician and client to have.

However, it is also true that clients will have to work hard, learn their DBT skills and use them in their daily lives. The both/and perspective here is that clients are doing the best they can with what they have and they absolutely have to work harder by using DBT skills to be more effective in their lives. Clinicians are encouraged to maintain an optimal balance using this philosophical foundation.

For example, a client comes to treatment and reports wanting his life to be better. The client engages in near daily non-lethal self-harm behaviors, which involve cutting and burning. Over the first two months of therapy, the clinician teaches assertiveness skills, illustrates the importance of self-care and focuses on reducing depressive symptoms. However, the client is still engaging in self-harm as a way to deal with his stress. The clinician is frustrated and feels hopeless because the client won't stop this problematic behavior. The therapy process is stagnated, and there is a lot of tension during sessions between the clinician and the client.

If the clinician can apply the philosophy that the client is doing the best he can and that he needs to learn DBT skills to be more effective in his life, then the therapeutic progress may be restarted. The first half of this dialectical balance requires both the clinician and client to recognize and accept that the client's behavior serves a function. It relieves stress, provides familiarity, and perhaps confirms the client's negative self-judgment. This behavior may also have been very useful in the client's chaotic and abusive family during his formative years. The client may have used this behavior to feel grounded, alive, and in control of something. Given the client's history, it makes sense that self-harm would be a reasonable behavior for a while. This stance is one of compassion and understanding, which is very useful for the clinician, the client, and the therapeutic relationship.

The other half of the dialectical balance comes after the clinician validates the client and then requires him to stop the self-harm behavior. The clinician explains that the goal of DBT is to build a life worth living. Continued self-harm or other destructive behaviors run contrary to this goal. While it may not be easy for the client to stop the self-harm behavior (otherwise he would have already done so), it is absolutely essential.

At this point the clinician selects DBT skills that help the client meet the same needs that were fulfilled by the self-harm behavior. By substituting other skills that fulfill the same needs, the client can replace the self-harm behavior. Some suggested skills for this might be *Nonjudgmental, Radical Acceptance, MEDDSS, FAST* or *Ride the Wave*, which are discussed in greater detail in Chapter 3. The client will learn and practice these skills. It is common to experience slips and relapses involving self-harm behavior along the way, which is dealt with by repeated recommitment to using the skills and to not engaging in self-harm. Ultimately the client dedicates himself to being as effective as he can be, which requires finding more effective ways to deal with stress.

Clients have not caused all their problems, and they have to solve them anyway

The statement above is true for everyone in the world. There are times when individuals create or contribute to their own problems, while there are other times when problems simply happen. This philosophical perspective gets clients out of the "victim" or "martyr" stance—even when there are terrible things in their histories—and empowers them to be effective right now.

Clients who get stuck in the mindset that things "shouldn't" have happened to them may feel the need to process their experiences excessively in hopes of making sense of, or understanding, their negative experiences. Some clients believe that if they can find a reason, or make sense of it, it won't be so bad. Unfortunately, whatever has happened—whether in the recent or distant past—can't be changed, and focusing on it excessively is unproductive. Spending a great deal of time reflecting on the past can get in the way of living in the here-and-now.

A clinical example of this situation often includes clients who were raped or sexually molested. They may spend years in therapy trying to figure out what they did wrong, how they may have encouraged the abuser, or wondering if they deserved what happened to them. Most of their time, energy, and attention is spent reliving the past with hopes of finding meaning in it and a reason for why it happened. Unfortunately, sometimes bad things happen to people for no apparent reason. Even though these clients did not cause their problems, they still have to solve them. This philosophical point supports clients in acknowledging the trauma, productively learning from it, and resolving it before moving back to living the majority of their lives in the present.

This DBT philosophy is also useful when clients have a faulty belief that if something is unfair, then it shouldn't apply to them. They may have a political, ethical, or legal perspective that things shouldn't be the way they are and, as a result, that they shouldn't have to comply with that requirement. Phrases such as: "Corporations are ripping people off, so I can steal things from them too," "It's not fair, so I'm just going to do what I want," "No one helped me when I needed it, so why should I help others now?" or "My parents abused me, so what if I hurt people physically? It happened to me, it can happen to them" may indicate a client holds this belief.

These clients can discuss for hours how their perspective applies to them because things shouldn't have happened or reality should be different than it is. There may even be a kernel of truth in their perspective or a bit of reality to their viewpoint, but the entitlement these clients bring to their perspective is ineffective. There are many things in life that are unfair. Sometimes people don't get what they want. This does not mean they should not be held responsible for their behavior or not be expected to act appropriately. Ultimately, clients haven't always caused their problems, and they have to solve them anyway and deal with any aftermath that ensues.

THE EMPIRICAL MODEL

Biosocial theory is the foundation used to create DBT. The biosocial theory states that clients with BPD are emotionally dysregulated and they have been chronically invalidated. This leads to emotional escape, avoidance behaviors and an inability to effectively manage dialectics.

At the core of the DBT model is the dialectical balance that it strikes between validation and change strategies. This dialectical stance is a "both/and" perspective instead of an "either/or" perspective—seeing reality as black and white along with a lot of shades of gray. Individuals with BPD and other clients often have a hard time viewing things from multiple perspectives, suspending the need to be right, and meeting competing needs—such as needing others and being self-sufficient at the same time. These clients tend to bounce back and forth between the two extremes, rather than finding balance in the middle.

By using dialectics, clients can move away from the extreme viewpoints of "always/never," "good/bad," "me/you" and "win/lose." Instead, dialectics allows them to adopt a both/and perspective. Dialectics such as: letting go while maintaining control, making mistakes without shame and guilt, investing in relationships while taking care of self and accepting self, others, and the world as imperfect, help clients find balance.

DBT is an empirically-supported treatment (EST) for BPD and other difficult-to-treat diagnoses. It is a comprehensive model ultimately designed to empower clients to build a life worth living (Linehan, 2015). DBT is highly organized and includes the following components:

- Four core skills modules: Mindfulness, Distress Tolerance, Emotion Regulation and Interpersonal Effectiveness
- Learning and using skills in each of these areas
- Balancing validation and change strategies through dialectics
- Reciprocal and irreverent communication
- Increasing skill use through diary cards
- Reducing problem behavior through chain analysis
- Decreasing therapy-interfering behaviors on the part of clients and clinicians
- Clinician use of skills to build resiliency in the work
- Phone coaching to encourage generalization of the skills
- A consultation team to provide support and accountability to the clinicians

THE FIVE COMPONENTS OF DBT

Comprehensive DBT involves five different components:

Components	Function or Purpose
1. Skills Training	Enhance Capabilities to Change
2. Individual Therapy	Enhance Motivation to Change
3. Phone Coaching	Ensure Skills Generalization in Clients' Lives
4. Team Consultation	Enhance the Capabilities and Motivation of the Clinician
5. Ancillary Treatment	Structure the Environment to Support Clients and Clinician

Swales & Heard, 2016

Skills training gives clients strategies and tools to manage stress, frustration and crises. These strategies provide effective relationship skills, as well as learning to be in the here-and-now—since the past is the past and the future isn't here yet, the only thing any of us have an influence over is the present moment.

In the traditional DBT model, skills training occurs in a psychoeducational group therapy setting, which provides a very robust way of learning skills. Clients are taught skills from each of the four skills modules and sessions are structured like a class with homework assignments to facilitate the use, and practice, of skills in daily life. However, skills can also be taught in individual sessions, through phone support, and during outreach sessions in the community.

The purpose of skills training is to provide tools to foster resilience and replace problem behaviors with more effective behaviors. Some skills can work as a replacement strategy—instead of engaging in the problem behavior, clients can use their skills to cope, tolerate, and soothe themselves. Skills can also be taught as a prevention method—the regular use of these skills helps manage stress and decrease the likelihood of problem behaviors occurring in the first place.

Because skills are better understood if practiced, individuals will get the most out of the skills if they practice them on a regular basis, particularly before they really need them. The more the skills are used, the more likely they are to become second nature to the individual, and the more easily accessible they'll be when needed. All skills are designed to be used to build a life worth living through prosocial, healthy behaviors and relationships.

DBT AND STAGES OF CHANGE

Something to keep in mind when teaching skills is the client's "Stage of Change" (SOC). If clients are in the *pre-contemplation stage*, then they believe they don't even have a problem in the first place, so using skills seems unnecessary to them. When clients are in the *contemplation stage*, they have a lot of ambivalence about changing and they are unlikely to use new skills. If clients are in either of these two stages, it is recommended to forgo teaching new skills.

Instead, it is more effective to catch these clients when they are already being skillful in their lives, and to point out to them that they are using DBT skills without even realizing it. Given that these clients may have never even heard of DBT skills, this will be an opportunity to talk with these clients about being skillful and how DBT can help reduce problematic behaviors. Giving these clients credit for being skillful supports their self-efficacy and increases their "buy-in" to try new and different strategies, such as other DBT skills.

If clients are in the *preparation* or *action stages* of change, then they are already actively using DBT skills and letting go of problematic behaviors and strategies. The next task is to help these clients achieve the *maintenance stage*, where the skills become a regular part of their lives and they engage in little to no problematic behavior.

One thing that can get in the way of this process is the *relapse stage*. Relapse occurs when an individual resorts to old behavior and stops using recently learned skills. This can occur for a variety of reasons, including if they become complacent or bored with skills, have a significant life change occur, are under enormous stress, or experience an unexpected crisis. It's important to note that everyone relapses or drifts back to old behavior from time to time. It's not a fault, but an opportunity to learn how to be more skillful in more sophisticated ways, use skills in more life domains, or use skills more regularly.

BUILDING MOTIVATION

Individual therapy is where clients build the motivation to change. Change can be hard, uncomfortable, and sometimes misunderstood. In this process, it is often helpful to explore change in terms of four quadrants that acknowledge the positives and negatives associated with changing versus staying the same:

Positives of staying the same	Negatives of changing
Negatives of staying the same	Positives of changing

Exploring the positives of staying the same and the negatives of changing validates the client and helps to explore what gets in the way of change. After all, if everything about the client's behavior were negative, then they wouldn't engage in the behavior in the first place. Similarly, if everything about their behavior were positive, then they wouldn't need DBT. An important aspect of this exploration is the opportunity to identify the benefits of staying the same to see if they can be met in alternative, healthier ways. Another part of this process is eliminating barriers to change. What gets in the way of change? Does the client need more knowledge? Do they need more practice? Do they need to break the process into smaller steps? Would changes in social support be helpful?

Another aspect of individual therapy is providing support to the client, which involves processing day-to-day and historical struggles. The skills group does little processing to prevent clients from becoming unintentionally triggered and to prevent them from receiving positive reinforcement for problematic behavior. Dealing with trauma and all of its layers is best done in individual therapy. Similarly, other mental health concerns and addiction issues are dealt with in individual therapy. In the traditional DBT model, individual therapy happens up to four times a week.

Phone coaching helps clients generalize using their skills beyond the therapy room. Clients access their clinicians via phone when they are dealing with day-to-day stressors and crises. If they become triggered to engage in problematic behaviors, they call their therapists before engaging in those behaviors. The therapists then coach the clients to use skills in that moment to more effectively manage the stress and disengage from the triggers to act problematically. Phone coaching is an excellent way for clients to interrupt their destructive processes and replace these behaviors with more prosocial skills, which leads to clients being more effective in their lives. For clients who need this level of support, phone coaching is a great service.

Many non-intensively trained DBT therapists find this component of the model cumbersome and believe that it has the possibility of fostering dependence. While many intensively-trained therapists say that clients don't typically over-utilize this intervention, it can still weigh heavily on the treating therapist. Clients may interpret phone coaching as evidence they don't have the answers and can't solve their own problems or take care of themselves. There are also certain settings where having after-hours contact with the treating therapist is inappropriate and/or prohibited, such as state hospitals, correctional institutions and residential programs. Additionally, homeless clients and clients with low incomes might also have limited phone access, making phone coaching impractical for them.

There can be many barriers to implementing this mode of DBT. Fortunately, there are also many alternative ways to achieve the same purpose without relying on phone coaching. This will be discussed in the "Customizing DBT" section later in this chapter.

Team consultation is the equivalent of group supervision with a specific DBT structure. The purpose of this component is to provide motivation for the clinicians to stay the course of DBT treatment and remain engaged with clients. It is about increasing the competency of all team members through discussions, shared readings and case consultations. The consultation team provides clinicians with support and accountability as they discuss challenges with a client, complications in treatment and countertransference. Team members can also help the clinician remain in balance and maintain a dialectical stance.

Every DBT clinician on the consultation team uses the skills in their lives to stay connected to their work, as well as to avoid negativity and burnout. One of the most powerful DBT skills for clinicians to use is *Nonjudgmental*. This skill helps the team and the clinician judge behavior as problematic or functional, but avoids judging the client or the clinician as "good" or "bad." When clinicians use this DBT skill on a regular basis in their daily lives, it builds an enormous amount of resiliency.

There are six conditions DBT consultation teams agree to remember:

1. **The biosocial theory** underlies the philosophical underpinnings of DBT, which maintains that we are all doing the best we can and we can be more effective by learning and using our DBT skills.

2. Treatment is designed through **consultation with the client.** This process entails actively talking with clients about their treatment progress and their goals. It means we advocate for the client even if we disagree with them. Whenever possible, the client is included in discussions with the team, family members, primary care physicians and other healthcare professionals. This approach empowers the client to state their needs and form working relationships with these individuals. It also dramatically decreases judgmental conversations that can occur when the client is not present in the discussion. If a clinician wouldn't say something to the client, then it shouldn't be said to anyone else.

3. **Strive for consistency while realizing it is imperfect.** This is a core dialectic. Consistency is always a little imperfect. As clinicians and a treatment team, we all have moments and days when we are more flexible or more rigid. We all have times when we are impatient and short-tempered. Having compassion for our team members and ourselves helps us implement this team agreement. None of us are perfect, and sometimes the best learning comes from mistakes.

4. **Clinicians work within their limits.** Everyone in life has limits, including clinicians. We can't be all things to all people at all times; and if we don't take care of ourselves, we may not be able to take care of anyone else. As mental health professionals, we witness a lot of pain and suffering. We may be vicariously traumatized by the life circumstances we hear about when terrible things happen to clients, or they engage in life-threatening behaviors toward themselves and destructive behaviors toward others. As a result, clinicians need to take care of themselves both at work and away from work. Working within our limits can take many forms, such as limiting the number of high-acuity clients on our caseload, structuring phone coaching to occur during specific times/days or by certain amounts each week and scheduling a break between intense clients. Unfortunately, working within limits can be challenging in some work environments where there are productivity expectations or crises walk in the door without advanced warning or with regularity, but it is important nonetheless.

5. **Remain nonjudgmental of the client and oneself.** Being able to separate the value of the person from the behavior allows us to effectively evaluate the behavior (e.g., is it helpful or unhelpful?), not the person. Clients are doing the best they can based on their internal strengths and weaknesses, and their environmental influences. Because of their circumstances, it makes sense that they are who they are and that they do what they do. This reality encourages us to be nonjudgmental, compassionate, and humble. Our job is to understand this and help them become more effective and prosocial in pursuit of a life worth living. Not only do we need to be nonjudgmental toward clients, we should also strive to be nonjudgmental with ourselves and our teammates. We can focus on improving our behavior and being more effective as clinicians; however, mistakes, missteps and errors don't make us bad clinicians or bad people.

6. **Accept that everyone is fallible and makes mistakes sometimes.** This goes hand-in-hand with being nonjudgmental. Being nonjudgmental is always easier if we can remember we are fallible and everyone makes mistakes. Of course, no one is perfect—although we may strive for perfection—so being forgiving and compassionate to ourselves, teammates, clients and their families is crucial.

Consultation teams typically start by engaging in a mindfulness exercise, reviewing the six agreements by reading them aloud, and then setting an agenda that is collaboratively agreed upon. This consultation helps to maintain fidelity of the DBT model and to ensure the hierarchy of target behavior is triaged appropriately. DBT calls for issues to be addressed in the following order:

1. Life-threatening behavior

2. Therapy-interfering behavior

3. Behaviors that reduce quality of life

4. Increasing functioning through use of skills

5. Dealing with any trauma issues

6. Increasing self-respect

7. Working on individual goals

Because DBT clients can be high-need, challenging clients who sometimes seem to get worse instead of better, it is essential that clinicians stay in balance, invest in their clients, and take care of themselves. A significant part of this process includes avoiding the anti-DBT tactics outlined at the end of this chapter.

Ancillary treatment is the fifth and final component of DBT, which involves working with primary care providers, other healthcare professionals, and the clients' support systems. Ancillary treatment includes educating these individuals and support systems about the DBT framework, discussing how the client is utilizing DBT, and asking them to help support this work. We ask the support system to positively reinforce healthy, functional behavior while ignoring, when possible, less functional or immature behavior. An example is providing encouragement to clients when they are taking care of themselves, and not taking care of them when they are acting damaged or impaired. We ask healthcare professionals to stay calm and avoid escalating crises; and we ask prescribers not to over-medicate clients and, in particular, to consider not prescribing opiates, benzodiazepines or stimulants. In this component, we want to use the "consultation with the client" strategy by working with clients on how to effectively collaborate with healthcare professionals and their support systems.

THE SKILLS MODULES

The four skills modules of DBT are *Mindfulness, Distress Tolerance, Emotion Regulation,* and *Interpersonal Effectiveness.* Within each of these four categories are several skills that clients learn, practice and use in their lives.

In the traditional DBT model, clients participate in group and individual therapy every week, where they learn and practice skills. Most weeks, clients are also assigned homework to facilitate using their skills in their daily lives as much as possible. Clients are asked to track how often they use their skills on diary cards, which are reviewed at the start of each session. In addition, if a client engages in problematic behaviors instead of utilizing skills, clinicians help clients engage in chain analyses to determine how they could have used skills to reduce or eliminate the problem behavior.

Mindfulness

	Being present in the here-and-now in a nonjudgmental fashion.
Be Mindful	Be mindful of using my skills, engaging in self-care, having healthy fun and connecting to my support system.
Effectively	Be as effective as I can in my life.
Mindful Eating	Focus on eating and chew each bite fully. Notice the complexity of the food, the sensations of fullness and satiation.
Moment to Pause	Take a quick moment to check in with myself on the inside, outside and in my interactions.
Nonjudgmental	Suspend evaluations about myself and others.
Observe, Describe & Participate	Just notice. Become aware of things in this one moment. I will describe my experiences in concrete, specific terms that are nonjudgmental. Engage fully and completely in each activity.
ONE MIND	**O**ne thing at a time, be in the **N**ow and grounded in the **E**nvironment. Stay in the **M**oment, **I**ncrease my awareness of my five senses, be **N**onjudgmental and **D**escribe what is going on.
Square Breathing	Breathe in while counting to four, hold it for four seconds, then exhale while counting to four. Repeat four times.
Turtling	Take care of myself like a turtle. Retreat inside for safety sometimes, go slowly and methodically, protect myself but don't be aggressive, be adaptive in a variety of situations, use my hard outer shell to let others' judgments roll off my back and get myself back in balance persistently.
Wise Mind	Balancing Rational Mind and Emotional Mind to be as skillful as I can be in *Wise Mind*.

Distress Tolerance

	Effectively managing frustrations, stressful situations and crises.
ACCEPTS	Distract myself with **A**ctivities, **C**hoices, **C**ontributions, **E**motions, **P**ushing away, **T**houghts and **S**ensations.
Crisis Survival Network	Create a list of people who support me and use it flexibly.
Half Smile	Find something in my day or life I can have a genuine *Half Smile* about.
IMPROVE	Distract myself with **I**magery of a beautiful or safe place, find **M**eaning in my life, **P**rayer, **R**elaxation, **O**ne thing at a time, **V**acation from the demands of my life and **E**ncouragement to be effective.
Keeping It In Perspective	Because of everything I have been through, I am able to effectively deal with my life and what is happening to me.
Radical Acceptance	Focus on what I have control of: my thoughts, feelings, impulses and behaviors. Let go of things I can't control: others and the world around me.
Self-Soothe Kit	Create a kit that is self-soothing and use it when needed.
SPECIFIC PATHS	What is my **S**upreme concern? **P**ractice my skills, focus my **E**nergy and **C**oncentration, **I** can be effective, have **F**aith, consider what is **I**mportant, have **C**ourage and **P**atience, pay **A**ttention, complete **T**asks, be **H**umble and have **S**ensitivity.
Turning the Mind	I am in the driver's seat; I can drive down an effective path of thinking, feeling and behaving.
Willingness	I can practice *Willingness* to accept reality, a bad day, things not going my way or that I can't control others and the world around me.

Emotion Regulation

Managing day-to-day emotions and impulses well.			
ABC	**A**ccumulate positives	**B**uild mastery	**C**ope ahead
BEHAVIOR	Use effective **B**ehavior, be grounded in the **E**nvironment, do things that are **H**ealing not hurting, **A**ct in my best interest, be consistent with my **V**alues, **I**magine getting through difficulties, focus on the desired **O**utcome and **R**einforce my successes.		
CARES	Manage my emotions by being **C**alm, monitoring **A**rousal, finding **R**elaxation and rest, coping with my **E**motions and getting a healthy amount of **S**leep.		
EMOTIONS	**E**xposure to emotions, **M**indful of current emotions, **O**utline a plan to deal with emotions, **T**ake opposite action, **I**ncrease positive experiences, identify **O**bstacles and plan to overcome them, **N**otice what is going on and use my **S**upport system.		
Feeling Not Acting	Use my *Moment to Pause* skill to identify and feel my impulses or urges. I can choose to use a skill to manage it or to tolerate it while doing nothing.		
Lemonade	Refocusing my weaknesses so they become strengths.		
Love Dandelions	Build an awareness and acceptance of parts of myself I find unattractive or don't like. I can manage these things effectively so they don't cause me distress.		

MEDDSS	**M**astery	**E**xercise	**D**iet	**D**rugs (prescriptions)	**S**leep	**S**pirituality

Opposite to Emotion	Engage in the action that will bring the opposite emotion into my awareness to balance the distressing emotion.
Ride the Wave	Imagine I am riding the wave of my emotions and impulses while not acting on them.

Interpersonal Effectiveness

Getting wants and needs met while sustaining healthy, functional relationships along with maintaining a sense of self, and an ability to set appropriate boundaries and be appropriately assertive.	
4 Horsemen of the Apocalypse	Identify the four most destructive things I bring into my relationships. Be skillful to keep these things out of my relationships.
Broken Record	Be a broken record with myself. Keep coming back to my needs.
Dealing with Difficult People	Be nonjudgmental, participate in improving my relationship, and identify and overcome obstacles to improvement.
DEAR SELF	**D**escribe what I want, be **E**ncouraging, **A**sk for what is wanted and **R**einforce others. **S**ometimes tolerating not getting my way, **E**xperiencing the present moment mindfully, inside and outside my body, **L**istening skillfully to myself and others and **F**inding negotiation opportunities.
FAST	Be **F**air to myself, **A**pologize less, **S**tick to my values and be **T**ruthful with myself.
GIVE	Be **G**entle, **I**nterested and **V**alidating and have an **E**asy manner with others.
Relationship Assumptions	I and others are doing the best we can, and we can work on being more effective. None of us have caused all our problems, and yet we need to solve them anyway.
Relationship Mindfulness	Identify generalizations, describe assumptions, suspend judgments, avoid jumping to conclusions and be empowered in my relationships.
Repairs	I can apologize, accept apologies and let some things go to be skillful in relationships.
Turn the Tables	Be reciprocal. Do things for other people without the expectation of getting anything in return.

VALIDATION AND CHANGE STRATEGIES

Clinicians must strike a dialectical balance between validation and change strategies to engage the client in DBT at the beginning of treatment, as well as throughout the process. Validation creates safety and fosters the therapeutic relationship. Given that most clients have grown up in, and perhaps still live in, invalidating environments, validation from a clinician can provide a corrective emotional experience. From the validation of the clinician, clients can learn to validate and trust themselves. This can lead to increased confidence, empowerment and self-efficacy. The six levels of validation are:

1. **Stay Awake and Engaged**

   The first thing that communicates caring and engagement is being psychologically and emotionally present with an individual. Being distracted or falling asleep sends the opposite message. Too many clients have commented that previous mental health professionals have done one or both of these things. There is no way to say to someone, "I care so much about you I fell asleep while you were talking." Our unchecked countertransference or reactions to the client can be equally as disengaging as falling asleep. Both of these scenarios emphasize the importance of clinician self-care, utilizing skills and knowing one's limits.

2. **Reflective Listening**

   Reflective listening is a foundational skill in psychotherapy and is now being used across the spectrum of health services. Although it is foundational, it is easy to forget to use it. Reflective listening requires reflecting back to the client what they have said, the tone of their voice, and their nonverbal communication. It's like being a mirror to their thoughts, emotions and behaviors. At times, it is possible to make an inaccurate reflection or reflect something that shifts the client's meaning when you restate it.

   When this happens, the client may correct the reflection. At this point, reflecting their new sentiment demonstrates that the clinician is attending to the client and working with the client's perspective, even when it shifts. While it seems like a simple intervention, it is very powerful. Psychotherapy is one of the few situations where clients can experience being the sole focus. Many clients have been invalidated and told to feel differently, think differently, and act differently. When these clients experience reflective listening, they feel incredibly validated, heard, and understood. Continually reflecting their feelings, thoughts, and actions affirms that their reality is real for them and that they are doing the best they can.

3. **Verbalize Unspoken Emotions**

   Some clients have learned to suppress their emotions, while others are out of touch with their emotions—although it is clear they are having emotions when they are talking about their lives. In these cases, a clinician can label the unspoken emotions, provide psychoeducation about emotions, and share that although the emotions aren't good or bad, the behavior that the emotions propel may be problematic. Using a process similar to that involved in exposure to some feared stimuli, clinicians work with clients to get them more and more comfortable feeling, tolerating and coping with the full range of emotions. For many individuals, an emotions vocabulary is often limited to a few words (e.g., happy, mad, sad, scared, etc.), so clinicians may need to help clients build up their emotions vocabulary so they can more accurately recognize and label their emotional experiences.

4. Validate Based on Learning and Past Experience

Many clients are survivors of trauma, mental health concerns, addictions, poverty, catastrophes, oppression, racism, and other "isms." Clients have learned how to survive. They haven't always been successful, and sometimes they may have made situations worse than they needed to be; and yet, they have gotten through it. Perhaps they are still dealing with situations or issues, and they are doing the best they can. This validation strategy is about letting clients know that they are doing the best they can and that they are surviving based on the strategies they have learned from their previous life experiences. Acknowledging the adaptations that the client has made as a result of their life experiences can be a powerful strategy to help build motivation to learn new and more effective skills offered through DBT, or to even identify areas where only slight modifications might drastically change their effectiveness.

5. Validate Based on Typical Functioning in the Current Context

At the same time that we are validating clients' survival skills and behaviors, we also want to validate when they are thinking, acting, or behaving effectively in their current lives. We should positively reinforce clients any time they demonstrate that they are taking care of themselves, engaging in healthy relationships and effectively managing their lives.

6. Radical Genuineness

In addition to the other five strategies, clinicians can be radically genuine with clients while still maintaining appropriate boundaries. This genuineness could happen in micro-communications where the clinician shares with the client that they might have felt the same way if they had experienced the same situation, or that the client's interpretations and reactions make sense to the therapist. The therapist can also use self-disclosure in small ways. For example, a therapist might share a similar loss or struggle without getting into too many details and taking the focus off the client. Like the other validation strategies, this one is very powerful and therapeutic.

Validating Thoughts, Feelings and Behaviors

Since clients with BPD have been chronically invalidated again and again, continued validation helps to restore balance. Another important part, however, involves using change strategies. It is not sufficient to just validate the clients, nor is it sufficient to only expect change. Not everything that clients are thinking, feeling or doing is functional and appropriate. Clinicians must balance their validation interventions with change strategies.

Therapeutic Dialectics	
Validation Strategies	Change Strategies
Six Levels of Validation	Contingency Management
Emotional Validation	Exposure
Cognitive Validation	Cognitive Restructuring
Behavioral Validation	Skills Training, Diary Cards, and Chain Analysis
Cheerleading	

Six Levels of Validation and Contingency Management

Clinicians can choose what and when to validate for the purpose of encouraging, reinforcing and rewarding change that leads to clients being more effective.

Emotional Validation and Exposure

Clinicians can also validate client emotions as real, and not as positive or negative, while also engaging in exposure techniques to decrease emotional avoidance. This approach increases the client's ability to manage, cope with and tolerate emotions without reverting to the problem behavior propelled by the intense emotions.

Cognitive Validation and Cognitive Restructuring

Clinicians can validate that the client's thinking makes sense given their life experiences, while picking and choosing dysfunctional thoughts to restructure. Not all thoughts are functional, so therapists help clients change and reorganize their thinking in a more effective manner for the client.

Behavioral Validation with Skills Training, Diary Cards, and Chain Analysis

A client's behavior serves some function (or they wouldn't engage in these behaviors to start with), and it can be made more effective through skills training, diary cards, and chain analysis. Skills training helps clients gain the skills needed to reduce or eliminate problem behavior. Diary cards help clients remember to use their skills and dramatically increase the number of times clients do so. Chain analysis helps clients learn how to use skills in targeted ways to specifically reduce or eliminate problem behavior. The clinician identifies, perhaps collaboratively with the client, the DBT skills that will most empower the client to improve their behavior, become more effective and increase functioning.

Cheerleading

After balancing all the validation and change strategies, clinicians are encouraged to continue cheerleading and positively reinforcing the client. Ongoing cheerleading is an effective antidote to the chronic invalidation many clients have experienced.

Components of DBT, and specifically the validation and change strategies, should be included in treatment planning.

COMMUNICATION AND COMMITMENT STRATEGIES

Irreverent and Reciprocal Communication

Irreverent communication is about being funny, poking fun at ourselves to model not taking ourselves so seriously, viewing life from alternative perspectives and focusing on what is most important to the client. It is designed to push the client out of their usual pattern of interactions and behaviors so they can consider different and unique options. Reciprocal communication is about being responsive, genuine, empathic, validating and using self-disclosure in service of a functional therapeutic relationship. Clinicians can balance these two types of communication for maximum benefit to the client and success of the therapy.

Validation and Commitment Strategies

Validation strategies involve supportive communication, reflective listening, cheerleading, and accepting the client's perception of reality. Validation lets clients know they are understood and appreciated for the individuals they are. Their experiences of reality are accepted as real for them, even if the clinician or others might not experience things the same way. Validation creates safety and fosters the therapeutic relationship.

However, clinicians should balance validating the client while gaining commitment to the treatment process. They need to provide enough of each strategy, while avoiding getting stuck in too much of either position.

DBT commitment strategies are dialectical strategies used to motivate the client to engage in treatment, increase their commitment to the DBT treatment process, and encourage the possibility of changing. These strategies include *Pros and Cons, Playing Devil's Advocate, Foot in the Door, Door in the Face, Linking Present and Prior Commitments, Freedom to Choose* and *Absence of Alternatives*.

- **Pros and Cons** is sometimes called a cost-benefit analysis or decisional balance. It helps the client consider whether change makes sense, and it helps them think through how they might change if they decide to do so. This process can be targeted at specific behaviors or decisions, or it can be used to consider engaging in DBT more generally.

Pros of continuing to use current skills, strategies and engaging in problem behavior	Cons of engaging in DBT, learning skills, practicing and using DBT skills and strategies
Cons of continuing to use current skills, strategies and engaging in problem behavior	Pros of engaging in DBT, learning skills, practicing and using DBT skills and strategies

- **Playing Devil's Advocate** is a strategy that is somewhat opposite to **Pros and Cons**. This strategy involves asking clients, "Maybe DBT isn't for you. What's the worst that could happen if you keep engaging in these same behaviors?" or "Are you sure you want to commit to DBT? Treatment is hard work, and you might want to quit when it gets hard." It might include best- and worst-case scenarios. This strategy encourages the client to make quick changes and commitments rather than getting stuck in thinking too much about it.

- **Foot in the Door** is a strategy that keeps clients engaged by not asking too much. It's about being supportive, understanding and engaged. This metaphor is based on the old traveling salespeople who would put a foot in the door to keep the conversation going with the potential buyer. For example, if a client says they don't want to talk about their homework, you might start by asking the client how their week (or day) has gone. This would allow the client to share something with you and potentially "open the door" to discussing other topics, such as homework.

- **Door in the Face** is a strategy that asks clients to do the hardest thing first. The metaphor is about closing the door on something that seems unreasonable so when a smaller or more reasonable-sounding request is made the client is more likely to agree to it.

- **Present Commitments** helps the client understand and follow through with obligations and commitments they have in their lives now, including commitments to the therapist and/or treatment team.

- **Prior Commitments** helps the client maintain their prior commitments to be safe, healthy and more functional. When a client has already spent time and energy learning DBT, it makes sense for them to stay on that path because it is consistent with their prior commitment to DBT.

- **Freedom to Choose** lets the clients know that the choice is up to them. There are a variety of choices they can make, including the choice to stay the same. Furthermore, there are positives and negatives to every choice, and refusing to make a choice is a choice in and of itself.

- **Absence of Alternatives** helps the client realize there are no other alternatives to improving their lives but to change, engage in therapy and use their DBT skills. They have tried many things, sometimes over many years, without the desired results. Having run out of options, the client might as well give DBT a try.

These commitment strategies work dialectically. Clinicians use *Pros and Cons* with *Playing Devil's Advocate* to get a client to simultaneously consider many details about engaging in DBT, while also throwing caution to the wind. *Foot in the Door* and *Door in the Face* balance making therapy easy and challenging. *Present and Prior Commitments* work hand-in-hand to help the client meet the obligations they make to themselves, their support system, their therapist, and the treatment team. Finally, *Freedom to Choose* and *Absence of Alternatives* emphasize that clients get to choose to make changes, while also acknowledging their previous choices have not gotten the desired results. All of these strategies are designed to increase engagement with DBT and the motivation to work hard, be imperfect and be open to new possibilities.

THERAPY-INTERFERING BEHAVIORS

Therapy-interfering behaviors are things that clients and clinicians do to interfere, derail, or damage the therapeutic process. It is essential to reduce or eliminate therapy-interfering behaviors from both clients and clinicians alike.

Clients and families do many things that get in the way of therapy, such as being late on a regular basis or not showing up for sessions at all, not doing homework or practicing skills, failing to complete diary cards, lying or omitting important information, derailing therapy with less important topics or waiting until the end of the session to talk about what's important, failing to pay fees, engaging in problematic behavior in and out of session and many more.

A variety of strategies can be utilized to deal with client therapy-interfering behaviors, including acknowledging and talking about these behaviors, using the informed consent effectively to make expectations of client responsibilities clear, leveraging the therapeutic relationship, tapping into the client's strengths and using behavioral contracting. In addition, clinicians may apply natural and logical consequences when appropriate, such as ending the session on time when the client is late, charging a no-show fee for missed sessions and conducting chain analysis before focusing on the client's desired topics.

Clinicians, and the treatment system, sometimes engage in therapy interference as well. Examples of this include not being physically or emotionally present in the session or answering the phone or checking email during the session, regularly starting sessions late or running over time, doing more talking than listening, being judgmental toward the client, allowing unchecked countertransference, failing to maintain effective boundaries, engaging in unhealthy codependency or getting personal needs met by the client and many more.

Clinicians can minimize these therapy-interfering behaviors by staying in balance in the relationship, practicing self-care, and utilizing supervision, consultation and peer support. In addition, it is helpful for clinicians to use DBT skills in their professional role and personal lives, as it reduces therapy-interfering behaviors and combats negativity and burnout. This also helps them become more knowledgeable about the skills so they are better able to assist clients and have more credibility when clients ask them how to use the skills in their lives.

Reducing or eliminating clinician-driven therapy interference can be facilitated by engaging in fewer anti-DBT tactics, while simultaneously increasing effective clinician characteristics and skills. The following list and worksheet should be used to help review the difference between anti-DBT tactics and effective clinician characteristics.

Therapy—Interfering Behaviors

Anti-DBT Tactics	Effective Clinician Characteristics and Skills
1. Call or think of the client as a manipulator.	1. Hold a balance of the client's strengths and areas for growth.
2. Communicate to the client how to feel, act or think.	2. Have a thorough knowledge of DBT skills.
3. Tell the client that other people should be different.	3. Develop stories and metaphors to facilitate skills training.
4. Tell the client what their feelings are.	4. Plan for the client to resist using skills and to resist staying the course of DBT.
5. Accuse the client of playing games or of not trying.	5. Role-play skills in session.
6. Accuse the client of playing staff off against each other, either directly or to other staff.	6. Assign skills practice as homework.
7. Criticize the client's feelings.	7. Review homework assignments.
8. Encourage the client to mask emotions, or reinforce attempts to escape or avoid emotions.	8. Provide coaching and encouragement for effective skills implementation.
9. Stress the irrationality or distorted basis of their feelings.	9. Be comfortable with ambiguity.
10. Use the clinician's interpretations to attack, blame or punish the client.	10. Empower clients.
11. Respond to painful feelings as something to get rid of.	11. Avoid viewing or talking about the client in negative terms.
12. Tell the client that problems are all in the mind.	12. Accept the client "as is" while encouraging change.
13. Oversimplify the client's problems, implying that all will be well.	13. Be centered and firm, while being flexible when appropriate.

14. Push a particular set of values or philosophy of reality and truth.	14. Establish clear limits of acceptable behavior.
15. Present a rigid view of events.	15. Adopt a non-defensive attitude.
16. Be judgmental of the client's choice of goals or commitments.	16. Help clients analyze factors that inhibit or interfere with effort and motivation.
17. Impose the clinician's goals on the client.	17. Manage therapeutic transitions effectively.
18. Be rigid about goals or procedures to reach goals.	18. Assist clients in managing change and things that are out of their control.
19. Be punitive.	19. Practice good self-care.
20. Require behaviors beyond the client's capabilities.	20. Effectively manage countertransference.
21. Operate in a non-collaborative manner.	21. Utilize supervision, consultation and therapy when needed.
22. When problem-solving, ignore what the client can do in the situation.	22. Practice DBT skills yourself.
23. Overload the client with information.	23. Foster dialectical thinking while compassionately confronting non-dialectical thinking.
24. Get into a power struggle with the client.	24. Suggest alternative ways of thinking and interpreting reality.

Identifying Anti–DBT Tactics
----Clinician Worksheet----

Use the following questions as a starting point for considering where and how anti-DBT tactics might come up in your workplace or organization, and then create a plan for overcoming them.

1. How can you as a clinician avoid anti-DBT tactics and achieve more effective clinician characteristics and skills?

   _____

   _____

   _____

   _____

2. How can you work with your colleagues and peers to avoid anti-DBT tactics and achieve more effective clinician characteristics and skills?

   _____

   _____

   _____

   _____

3. If working on a treatment team, how can members of the team avoid anti-DBT tactics and achieve more effective clinician characteristics and skills?

   _____

   _____

   _____

   _____

4. How can your agency or organization avoid anti-DBT tactics and achieve more effective clinician characteristics and skills?

   _____

   _____

   _____

   _____

CUSTOMIZING DBT

Limitations of ESTs

One significant criticism of using ESTs is that they are too difficult—or impossible—to fully implement in real-world settings. Such difficulties can be related to funding limitations, divergent staff backgrounds, productivity expectations, lack of proper training in the particular EST, or an inability to provide intensive clinical supervision focused on the EST. Another criticism of some ESTs is they have been normed on heterosexual, white, middle-class subject pools, which limits generalizability to diverse populations—including clients of different ethnicities, sexual orientations, gender identities or levels of socioeconomic status.

Additionally, clinicians in an individual practice are not typically working on a multidisciplinary team, so this may limit how much of the EST is implemented. For instance, many private practice clinicians do not offer group therapy; therefore, DBT is only offered in individual sessions. However, many clinicians who utilize DBT in this way report promising results for their clients nonetheless.

Intensively-trained DBT clinicians have expressed concerns that diverging from the DBT EST might do harm and be unethical. This concern has not been supported by any data. It is anticipated that graduate-trained clinicians holding licensure are meeting the ethical obligation to "do no harm" at the very minimum.

Possible Modifications

It is possible to adapt DBT to fit your clients and setting while remaining close to the EST. At its core, DBT is about clients learning to be more skillful in their lives: being in the here-and-now most of the time with an ability to manage emotions, tolerate distress, and be effective in their relationships; while also being nonjudgmental with self and others, and being as effective as possible in their lives. Since the goal of DBT is for the clients to build a life worth living, this would include stopping problematic, dangerous and unhealthy behaviors.

With all of this in mind, clinicians should be able to modify DBT to fit the needs of their clients and work within any limitations imposed by a setting or financial situation. Some areas for modification include: phone coaching, mindfulness, diary cards, individual therapy only, combining DBT with other treatments, and reworking skills to fit cultural or other diversity considerations of clients.

Phone Coaching

Phone coaching may be one of the most common components of DBT that is not implemented. Phone coaching is particularly helpful with clients who over-utilize the acute care system because they can call their clinician when they are in distress and at risk of harming themselves or engaging in other problem behaviors. This helps the client use their skills in a moment of crisis rather than self-harming or engaging in destructive behavior. For other clients with less severity, this component may not be necessary. Given that phone coaching is a 24/7 responsibility that cannot be implemented in all settings, it is possible to practice DBT without it. However, there are also alternatives.

Crisis lines can be an alternative to phone coaching, since they can provide some of the coaching if the crisis line staff are familiar with DBT. Another alternative to phone coaching includes clients getting involved in 12-step meetings. There are many 12-step meetings that have nothing to do with substances or that do not require an attendee be the one identified with a substance-use problem. One group that might be particularly helpful for clients who receive DBT treatment is Emotions Anonymous. Another option is Al-Anon. Individuals in 12-step meetings often have a sponsor who is available for phone and face-to-face support. Although the sponsor may not be familiar with DBT or clinically trained, the client can educate their sponsor.

If a client is not in a 12-step program, other community support meetings can be helpful. Self-Management and Recovery Training (SMART Recovery) is based on both CBT and Rational Emotive Behavior Therapy (REBT) and has tools like those offered in DBT. For example, *Pros and Cons* is referred to as a Cost-Benefit Analysis in SMART. In addition to face-to-face meetings, SMART offers online groups with voice and text options, which increase accessibility of support. Other ideas for support and coaching between therapy sessions include mentors, advisors, healthy family members and prosocial friends.

Mindfulness Doesn't Have To Include Meditation or Spirituality

Mindfulness can be connected to a spiritual practice or religious tradition, and can also be connected to regular meditation practice. If these fit for the clinician and client, then it is fine to include these components in DBT. However, it is possible to be mindful without spiritual, religious or meditative practices, and DBT itself does not require a religious or spiritual connection to use mindfulness. Mindfulness is about being present with oneself on the inside, aware of one's thoughts, feelings, and impulses. It is also about being present in the environment around oneself and in any interactions happening in the moment. Mindfulness also includes being connected to the past and future, without getting too caught up in either.

Reworking Skills

An area for DBT adaptation is reworking skills. Skills can be changed to make them more accessible to a client. An example of this is the skill of *Broken Record*. In the EST, *Broken Record* is being steadfast in relationships by clients stating their needs and wants again and again. Sometimes being a broken record starts to sound "whiny," may annoy others and prevents the client from using more effective strategies to meet a need. Instead, *Broken Record* can be turned inside. Clients can be a *Broken Record* with themselves. They can keep coming back to who they want to be in relationships and the life they want to have, and they can use this information to choose additional DBT skills to better attain that vision. Using the skill in this way can build motivation to change while also encouraging clients to do what is most effective.

Another reworking of skills is changing what a letter stands for in a particular acronym. Sometimes skills may not be appropriate based on the client's diverse makeup and will need modification. For example, in the acronym of IMPROVE, the "P" is for **Prayer**. This can be formal prayer or informal prayer; however, some clients reject the idea of prayer. In this case, the "P" can be changed to something else, such as **P**articipate fully, **P**lease help, or be at **P**eace. Another example is in the skill FAST, where the "A" stands for **A**pologize less. In some cultures, not apologizing (or apologizing less) would be offensive and inappropriate. There are also gender differences regarding apologizing in U.S. society, with females tending to be socialized to apologize even when they are not responsible for something and males being socialized to believe apologizing is a form of showing weakness which should be avoided. "Apologize appropriately" might make more sense to make this particular skill more accurate and useful for some clients.

Additionally, if the clients do not like the traditional DBT acronyms, they can create their own. When clients create their own acronym, they will remember it more easily, have a sense of pride because they created it, and use it more often since it is more on-target for their situation. Furthermore, while DBT contains many acronyms, it is entirely possible to practice DBT and teach clients skills without using any of the acronyms. Clinicians may also find that a client needs a skill not contained in the traditional DBT model. In these cases, innovative skills can be found in texts and online.

Diary Cards

Diary cards are designed to reinforce the client's use of the skills. Clients are asked to track how often they use the skills each day, including what specific skills they used. They also use diary cards to rate the severity of their emotions, impulses, and behaviors each day. Although diary cards help reinforce skill use, both clients and clinicians find them difficult to complete on a regular basis. However, both clients and clinicians will see more of a benefit from DBT if diary cards are used in some form or fashion to track skill usage. In an effort to simplify the diary card process, it can be helpful to have the client simply focus on counting the skills they use each day. This can be done on an index card, in a day planner, or electronically on their phone. When clients pay attention to their skill use and frequency, they will end up using their skills more often.

Therapy Delivery Method

In traditional DBT, clients attend a two-to-three hour skills training group, have individual therapy sessions, and engage in phone coaching. However, group therapy may not be an option for the clinician, and many clients are not interested in participating in groups for a wide variety of reasons. It is possible to deliver DBT through individual therapy only, which can be accomplished in a number of ways. Skills can be taught as part of the session on a weekly, bi-weekly, monthly, or as-needed basis. Role-plays and worksheets can also be completed as part of this process. In addition, clients can learn about completing diary cards between sessions, and chain analysis can be completed in session and as homework.

DBT can be combined with other therapeutic modalities as well. For instance, psychodynamic clinicians can use DBT for initial symptom management and to establish stability before delving into deep intrapsychic issues. DBT can be combined with CBT, since both models fall under the same treatment umbrella; and many clinicians use DBT and EMDR together. DBT can also be used with Gestalt and process therapies by helping the clients to be skillful while staying in the flow of the therapy. Additionally, addictions treatment programs provide the Matrix Model and DBT in combination. DBT can be used with other empirically-supported treatments as well.

All of these suggestions are shared to generate ideas and empower clinicians to make the DBT model work for them. Clinicians can choose to use these modifications, or find other ways to adapt DBT in a manner that works for them, their clients, and the settings in which they practice.

Chapter 2

Being Dialectical

One thing that is entirely unique about DBT is the focus on being dialectical. Dialectics are about holding in balance things that seem to be contradictory, mismatched or in conflict with each other. Ironies and paradoxes are solved through dialectics. Dialectics acknowledge that reality is black, white and many shades of gray; that there are times when there is more than one right answer, and other times when there is no single right answer. It is a both/and perspective.

Life is full of inconsistencies and contradictions. However, both clients and clinicians can learn to think and act dialectically, and work toward balance in a variety of ways. Balance is often about moving away from the extreme ends of the dialectic toward the middle, sometimes even blending a little bit of both ends of the spectrum. Furthermore, DBT provides many formal dialectics that clients try to find balance with, along with therapeutic dialectics the clinician is responsible for keeping in balance.

CLIENT DIALECTICAL DILEMMAS

Here are some of the most common dialectics clients face, along with suggested skills:

- Don't want to be in pain and don't want to change

- Believe reality is out of their control, while continuing to engage in controlling behavior

- Want their lives to be better while still engaging in problematic, self-destructive behaviors

- Want life to be easy and spend a lot of energy making it harder than it needs to be

- Demand respect while being disrespectful to others (and/or self!)

- Want to be treated like an adult while behaving in immature ways

- Focus on self and focus on others

- Want help and reject support

- Want spontaneity while life is full of obligations

- Balance reactivity and responsivity

Don't want to be in pain and don't want to change

Clients are often trying to avoid pain or trying to have less chaos in their lives. Unfortunately, some of their strategies are less than effective and don't produce the results they want. Frequently, the very thing they don't want to do will provide them with some of the results they are looking for. For example, clients with substance use disorders often hope to find a way to have better relationships and success with their careers while learning to control or moderate their use rather than giving it up. While some clients can learn to use moderately, many cannot.

For clients with out-of-control addictions, because of their biopsychosocial etiology, abstinence is recommended. These clients will be unlikely to achieve relationship or career success without abstinence. The more they try to control their use, the more control it has over them and the further away from their goals they find themselves. Instead, these individuals will come closer to their goals only when they abstain completely. That said, with initial abstinence, things often get worse before they get better because the client often must deal with the wreckage of their addiction.

Another example might be teenagers who experience interpersonal drama. Teenagers have a sense of loyalty and want to trust their friends and rely on their relationships. However, these same teenagers engage in gossip, indirect communication and being judgmental with one another, which is often disloyal, harms their relationships and typically results in emotional hurt or pain. The more teenagers engage in these behaviors, the more interpersonal drama and pain they will have, along with a decreased ability to rely on their relationships. Furthermore, when these friendships end or come to a critical moment, teenagers often continue this behavior of gossiping or being judgmental, blaming the other party instead of accepting responsibility for their part in the situation and changing their behavior. This pattern keeps them stuck in painful situations despite their desire for relief.

Taking a dialectical stance for the dilemma of wanting less pain while avoiding change can occur when clients learn how to tolerate, cope with and manage pain while also engaging in change strategies. Ultimately this may help clients manage their lives more effectively, increase their goal-directed behavior, and increase their overall level of functioning.

The following skills may be beneficial when working with clients who experience this dialectical dilemma:

> **Mindfulness:** Staying in the present moment.
> **Suggested Skill:** *Observe, Describe & Participate*
>
> **Distress Tolerance:** Building frustration tolerance in order to tolerate the pain, and becoming empowered to do things differently even when it is difficult or challenging.
> **Suggested Skill:** *Keeping It In Perspective*
>
> **Emotion Regulation:** Developing the ability to stay present with the emotions without engaging in problematic actions.
> **Suggested Skill:** *MEDDSS*
>
> **Interpersonal Effectiveness:** Staying connected to others even when in pain or stressed.
> **Suggested Skill:** *Turn the Tables*

Believe reality is out of their control while engaging in controlling behavior

Often clients feel their lives are out of control. These individuals view life as happening *to* them. They are passive—and perhaps even victims—of whatever happens to them. However, at the same time they engage in considerable controlling behavior. Controlling behavior can manifest in multiple ways, such as wanting things to be a certain way, believing that others should think the same way as them and investing a lot of energy in getting things their way, listening in on others' conversations or reading others' personal documents, watching others, over-interpreting cues in the environment, and enlisting allies to support their interpretations.

For example, a client might come in on a regular basis complaining that bad things keep happening to him, but he doesn't acknowledge that continuing to hang out with certain people will only lead to being taken advantage of. Other clients, who believe people are out to get them, sometimes try to protect themselves by engaging in intimidating behaviors, which may provoke others to attack them emotionally, interpersonally, or perhaps even physically.

Clients can learn to control what they do have control over: themselves. They can learn to manage their own thoughts, emotions, impulses and behaviors. They can learn to influence others and their environments, while investing most of their energy into their own thinking, feelings, impulses and actions. Letting go of their attempts to control others and the environment can empower clients to take better care of themselves by redirecting their energy away from things they are powerless over and toward the only thing they do have power over: themselves.

Working through the dilemma of being more in control without being controlling can be accomplished by clients accepting the fact that they have control over themselves and influence on others and the environment, while also accepting they can't control others or the environment. This balance empowers clients to focus their time, energy, and attention on managing their own lives effectively.

Some helpful skills for clients who experience this dialectical dilemma include:

Mindfulness: Being present with yourself—inside and outside—so you can focus your energy on effectively managing your life.
Suggested Skill: *Square Breathing*

Distress Tolerance: Learning to let go and move away from areas where you don't have influence. Being able to tolerate not getting your way all the time, and being curious about, and open to, unexpected positives that come from not getting your way.
Suggested Skill: *Radical Acceptance*

Emotion Regulation: Learning to cope with, and manage, emotions and impulses to build a life worth living.
Suggested Skill: *Feeling Not Acting*

Interpersonal Effectiveness: Investing in relationships even when you realize you cannot control how other people think, feel or behave.
Suggested Skill: *Relationship Assumptions*

Want their lives to be better while still engaging in problematic, self-destructive behaviors

Many clients come to treatment seeking help so they can have fewer problems and greater life satisfaction. They may present with ideas of what they want to work on, specific goals they want to make progress on, or they may even have a clear vision for their future. At the same time, many of these clients are unwilling to give up their problematic behavior. This behavior has helped them manage their chaotic, out-of-control lives. In extreme cases, clients have been using the problematic behavior as a survival strategy to manage their pain, distress, and dangerous environments for many years. In less severe cases, clients engaging in problematic behavior might minimize the damage and overestimate the benefits.

For example, clients with BPD who have a hard time tolerating psychological, emotional, and/or physical pain, may engage in self-destructive behaviors in an attempt to manage, distract, or deny the pain, or to create other pain. For these clients, clinicians recommend stopping the behaviors and replacing them with more functional coping strategies, which can often include one or more DBT skills.

However, in many cases, clients don't want to change their behavior; or they are unconvinced there might be something more effective for coping with, managing, reducing or eliminating their pain. Their self-destructive behaviors have been a survival strategy for managing their difficult or out-of-control life circumstances. These behaviors have been meeting a need despite their associated costs.

Other examples include clients who want to have better relationships with family members, but rage out of control; clients who actively engage in strategies to have fewer crises, while still cutting or burning themselves or making suicide attempts; or teenagers and young adults who work hard at school to plan a future, while withdrawing from relationships and failing to engage in effective self-care behaviors.

Balancing the dialectic of wanting life to be better while struggling to reduce or eliminate problematic behavior can occur by exploring the pros and cons of behavior, replacing the extreme behavior with more effective behavior, and appreciating the concerns others may have about their behavior. Key skills to incorporate for these clients are:

Mindfulness: Being in the here-and-now empowers you to deal with environmental and interpersonal realities.
Suggested Skill: *Moment to Pause*

Distress Tolerance: Utilizing the skills in this module provides many opportunities to be more effective, even in the midst of stress, drama and crisis.
Suggested Skill: *Half Smile*

Emotion Regulation: Being mindfully present with the impulse to engage in problematic behavior without acting on it. You can choose to tolerate the impulse or use skills to modulate it.
Suggested Skill: *Ride the Wave*

Interpersonal Effectiveness: You can use skills to balance objective, relationship and self-respect effectiveness in primary, intimate, and casual relationships.
Suggested Skill: *4 Horsemen of the Apocalypse*

Want life to be easy and spend a lot of energy making it harder than it needs to be

Some clients are hoping life will be easier, less stressful, and without problems. They would like to have less stress at work, school, home, in relationships, and perhaps even financially. Yet these same individuals make choices and behave in ways that make their lives harder than they need to be.

Examples of this include: a client who says they are committed to effectively managing stress, but who overcommits and doesn't leave sufficient time for adequate self-care; a client who desires less interpersonal drama in their life, but continues to gossip and talk negatively about co-workers or classmates; or a client whose self-characterization as "damaged" fuels their self-destructive behavior, but who talks about how being nonjudgmental of others has significantly improved relationships with family and friends.

Balancing the dilemma of wanting life to be easy, and yet engaging in behavior that makes things harder, can be accomplished by helping clients remember that while they're doing the best they can, they can also try harder, increase their skills, and be more effective.

Mindfulness: Staying out of the failures of the past or ruminating on the future empowers you to be more effective in the here-and-now. This is also facilitated by balancing immediate, short-term and long-term perspectives.
Suggested Skill: *Be Mindful*

Distress Tolerance: By being able to tolerate distress and frustration, clients can suspend the behaviors that make things worse.
Suggested Skill: *SPECIFIC PATHS*

Emotion Regulation: By combining Emotion Regulation and Distress Tolerance skills, you can learn that you have alternatives to patterns of ineffective behavior.
Suggested Skill: *EMOTIONS*

Interpersonal Effectiveness: By utilizing interpersonal effectiveness skills, you learn how to have healthy relationships.
Suggested Skill: *Relationship Assumptions*

Demand respect while being disrespectful

Everyone has a desire to be respected; and for some clients, this is extremely important. These individuals scrutinize the way others interact with them: the words spoken, the tone of voice, and other nonverbal cues. All of these are evaluated as being respectful or disrespectful. When a client determines they are being treated disrespectfully, they may react toward others or themselves in verbally or physically aggressive ways.

In addition, sometimes these same individuals behave in ways that are disrespectful to others—whether verbally or nonverbally. These behaviors can, in turn, cause others to respond in a way that the client perceives as disrespectful or provocative; which then encourages the client to engage in more of the same type of behavior, causing a vicious cycle of disrespect. In extreme cases, this becomes an escalating situation, which may end in threats, destruction of property or violence toward others.

Some examples include: a teenager who interprets another teen's tone of voice and eye contact as disrespectful and starts a physical altercation; or a client who feels disrespected at work and retaliates by choosing not to complete an assignment, which then results in team members being frustrated, less collaborative, and perhaps actively trying to discredit the client. Another example is a client who accuses their spouse of being disrespectful while the client uses negative, offensive and demeaning language to describe the disrespect.

Clients can balance the dilemma of expecting respect and tolerating disrespect while behaving respectfully, by paying attention to their own word choices, tone of voice, gestures, eye contact, and behavior, while also reducing or eliminating assumptions or interpretations of others' intentions or behaviors. Beneficial skills for these clients include:

Mindfulness: Staying grounded in the here-and-now internally, in your environment, and in interactions to avoid making interpretations or assumptions.
Suggested Skill: *Nonjudgmental*

Distress Tolerance: Learning to tolerate situations where disrespect has occurred.
Suggested Skill: *IMPROVE*

Emotion Regulation: Empowering yourself to be more effective by moving away from your own disrespectful behavior and ignoring the disrespectful behavior of others.
Suggested Skill: *Feeling Not Acting*

Interpersonal Effectiveness: Staying connected in relationships even if there has been disrespect on either side.
Suggested Skill: *Dealing with Difficult People*

Want to be treated like an adult while behaving in immature ways

While this may primarily apply to teenagers, it can also apply to children and even adults at times. In this situation, clients want to be treated like adults—being independent, making their own decisions and managing their own behavior. However, these same clients may have difficulty making decisions and be unable to regulate their impulses or modulate their emotions, which then interferes with their goal of being treated like an adult.

Some examples include teenagers who don't want their parents checking their online behavior, even though these teenagers are talking online to people they don't know and who might be unsafe; a young adult who stays out late in dangerous parts of town, but tells everyone that they are OK and can take care of themself; or a child who wants to be helpful to their parents and to be seen as a "big kid," but who bullies their younger siblings.

Balancing the paradox of wanting to be treated like an adult, but acting immaturely, can be achieved by learning to be assertive, engaging in appropriate behaviors, building confidence in oneself and earning confidence from others over time. Acknowledging that one doesn't have all the answers and being able to ask for help are important parts of being an adult as well. However, being able to have fun and not grow up too fast is also a major component of the process. Skills for these clients include:

> **Mindfulness:** Staying in the moment so you don't get ahead of yourself.
> **Suggested Skill:** *Square Breathing*

> **Distress Tolerance:** Effectively managing frustration tolerance and bouncing back from stressful situations are essential competencies for adulthood.
> **Suggested Skill:** *Self-Soothe Kit*

> **Emotion Regulation:** The ability to tolerate and cope with strong emotions and impulses is crucial for adulthood.
> **Suggested Skill:** *BEHAVIOR*

> **Interpersonal Effectiveness:** Adulthood is characterized by relationships that ebb and flow; some end, while others endure.
> **Suggested Skill:** *Repairs*

Focus on self and focus on others

Some clients spend most of their time and energy focusing on themselves, while other clients spend enormous amounts of time and energy focusing on others. Both perspectives are inherently out of balance. Other-focusing behavior may be evident when clients spend all their time taking care of partners or family members, but don't invest enough time in self-care, downtime, or having fun. They put their own needs on the back burner, doing favors and dropping everything to help someone else. Other clients may exhibit a self-focus by always expecting others to help them, but doing little for others. Self-focusing clients may also obsess about a particular component of their own lives, such as attractiveness, career or wealth.

It is entirely possible for clients to find a balance between focusing on themselves and others, as well as between giving and receiving. This might be thought of as healthy codependence, and it can be achieved by knowing oneself, being able to set limits and not allowing feelings of guilt to drive behavior into overdoing for others. For clients who struggle in this area, these skills are helpful:

> **Mindfulness:** Being in the here-and-now can empower you to stay grounded in your strategies to balance their focus on yourself and others.
> **Suggested Skill:** *ONE MIND*

Distress Tolerance: You can learn to manage your own needs and desires along with others' requests and demands.
Suggested Skill: *Keeping It In Perspective*

Emotion Regulation: Your ability to balance self and others, or giving and receiving, can require significant competency with Emotion Regulation.
Suggested Skill: *ABC*

Interpersonal Effectiveness: You can learn to achieve balance by investing in yourself and investing in relationships with others.
Suggested Skills: *GIVE* and *FAST*

Want help and reject support

Some clients communicate directly or indirectly that they need help, yet they often reject the assistance people offer. It may appear the client is generating a crisis and that any help offered by others is insufficient in the client's mind. In this situation, clients may feel invalidated because others don't understand the details of their lives and why the offered help will not work for them. Additionally, clients may interpret others' inability to help them as confirmation for some negative judgment about themselves, or a belief that they deserve to be miserable and in pain.

For instance, a depressed client's family members may suggest getting out of bed, being active and taking antidepressants, while in fact, the client feels incapable of doing even one of these things—let alone all three. The client and family members may also collude in the perceived hopelessness of the situation. Another client, struggling with addiction, may want to quit using substances, be free of pain and not disappoint their family. Yet they find reasons to pass up community supports, such as 12-step groups, drop out of a treatment program and begin hanging out with others who use drugs. Although this client may be very aware that this behavior puts their recovery at risk, that doesn't resonate with them, and they believe there is no other choice but to continue to use.

Balancing the dilemma of wanting help and having difficulty accepting it can be achieved by learning to sometimes accept help, even if it doesn't seem like it would be beneficial. Another component of this process involves learning to actively deal with a problem even when it can't be completely resolved. There may also be times when tolerating a painful situation is warranted; on these occasions, it is important not to request help from others, since the client has no intention of acting on help just yet. Skills that are useful for these clients include:

Mindfulness: The present moment provides an opportunity to decide what is really desired and to engage in the appropriate behavior, whether it is getting help to change or learning to be OK with the way things are.
Suggested Skill: *Turtling*

Distress Tolerance: You can learn to tolerate the fact that things don't always get better and that sometimes others want to help even when they aren't really helpful.
Suggested Skill: *Self-Soothe Kit*

Emotion Regulation: You can learn to stay grounded in life even when things don't seem to improve or when there are no useful answers.
Suggested Skill: *Feeling Not Acting*

Interpersonal Effectiveness: Being able to stay in relationships effectively without rejecting others is important for this skill set.
Suggested Skill: *DEAR SELF*

Want spontaneity while life is full of obligations

Many clients have a long list of obligations that demand most of their time, energy and attention. These same clients may crave spontaneity and want to have few or no obligations. Other clients have lots of spontaneity and live largely unstructured lives. These clients may experience life as ungrounded and having little meaning.

Balance occurs when clients have a mix of spontaneity and set obligations. For overburdened clients, it is important to reduce life obligations where possible. An essential part of this process may be accepting oneself, others and the world around them as imperfect; and also learning to say "no" and set appropriate limits. Clients with no structure and all spontaneity may need help finding meaning in structure and occasional hard work. Oftentimes even small increases in structure can help these clients feel more empowered and productive—which can feel counterintuitive to their preferred "spontaneous" lifestyle. The following skills are useful for clients on both ends of this spectrum:

> **Mindfulness:** Being in the moment with both obligations and spontaneity takes intentional mindfulness.
> **Suggested Skill:** *Be Mindful*

> **Distress Tolerance:** Managing the frustration and exhaustion of excessive obligations.
> **Suggested Skill:** *ACCEPTS*

> **Emotion Regulation:** Developing the ability to delay gratification.
> **Suggested Skill:** *Lemonade*

> **Interpersonal Effectiveness:** Empowering yourself to be present in your relationships while balancing demands.
> **Suggested Skill:** *Relationship Mindfulness*

Balance reactivity and responsivity

Some clients live their lives in a reactive manner. They often have crises—things just aren't going their way. They have learned to be hypervigilant so they can figure out what is going on and then react as quickly as possible. In these situations, clients will benefit from getting out of this reactive mindset. The ability to be responsive to life more often, rather than reactive, increases a client's effectiveness in a variety of domains.

Clients can balance reactivity, while still being responsive, by staying focused on what is going on internally and also externally and in their interactions with others, at the same time suspending the need to make assumptions, interpretations, reactions and judgments.

> **Mindfulness:** Staying in the moment helps you to remain grounded in your actual internal and external experiences, rather than in what you imagine is going on.
> **Suggested Skill:** *Wise Mind*

> **Distress Tolerance:** You can learn how to deal with difficulty and painful situations effectively.
> **Suggested Skill:** *Crisis Survival Network*

> **Emotion Regulation:** The impulse control fostered through these skills reduces reactivity.
> **Suggested Skill:** *Opposite to Emotions*

> **Interpersonal Effectiveness:** You can use these skills to establish self-respect and relationship effectiveness.
> **Suggested Skill:** *Broken Record*

DBT is about balance. It empowers clients to see that reality is black and white, as well as a lot of shades of gray. It also helps clients tolerate and manage the uncertainty of life; balance things that are contrary, confusing or in conflict, and yet are real or true for them (e.g., being independent versus being taken care of); and accept that life is imperfect, while taking control over what they can—their own thoughts, feelings, impulses and behaviors. Finding a dialectical balance is a process that happens both in intrapsychic and interpersonal ways, and also between the client and various environments.

CLINICIAN DIALECTICS

Clinicians also experience dialectics, both in their professional and personal lives. Below are a few examples that many clinicians have experienced at different points in their training and while providing clinical services:

- Using evidence-based practices while individualizing treatment
- Being culturally competent while using empirically-validated practices
- Remaining relationship-oriented while completing paperwork and insurance reviews
- Encouraging clients to engage in more effective self-care, while maintaining own sufficient self-care practices
- Diagnosing and seeing deficits, and having a strengths-based perspective
- Wanting clients to change, while not always being patient or positively reinforcing change
- Being critical of self, while being compassionate toward others
- Being committed to professional endeavors and investing in personal life
- Being competent while having a lifelong commitment to learning
- Wanting to be good at DBT before being ready to invest the time and energy to do so

Using evidence-based practices while individualizing treatment

The mental health and addictions fields have long been committed to providing individualized treatment. This requires collaboration with clients to understand their lives—including their difficulties and aspirations. Treatment planning and goal setting occur as the clinician and client get to know one another and agree upon steps in the treatment process.

Recently, there have been increasing mandates for clinicians, treatment centers, and human services agencies to utilize evidence-based practices (EBPs). EBPs are empirically-validated protocols shown to produce positive outcomes. These mandates require appropriate EBPs are used with the populations for whom they were designed and that they are applied in the same way as they were researched. Unfortunately, this process leaves little or no room for flexibility, creativity or individualization.

Many EBPs have a fidelity tool to assess how closely the treatment provided follows the research model. Often the fidelity tool includes direct observation of treatment services, interviews with clinical staff, program administrators and clients, as well as evidence in clinical documentation. Fidelity to the EBPs shows they are being implemented consistently. Funding sources and government oversight agencies are increasingly expecting and requiring fidelity to the EBPs, yet this is a stance that represents the opposite of individualized treatment.

It is still early in the field's development to strike a dialectical balance with these opposing attitudes. Some have written that it is essential to maintain the core components of EBPs, while being flexible enough to modify treatment when needed and build a strong therapeutic alliance. Using dialectics here is really about recognizing the shades of gray. The EBPs need to be recognizable and differentiated from other practices, while also meeting the client where they are, and including their goals and desires as integral components of the treatment process. Clinicians and supervisors must maintain vigilance to ensure this balance is achieved and maintained.

Being culturally competent while using empirically-validated practices

Another dialectic associated with the commitment to use EBPs is cultural competency. Most EBPs have been researched using participants from the dominant culture, which means participants were primarily Caucasian, middle class and heterosexual. Yet it is also important to understand and integrate a culturally-diverse perspective into the interventions and services provided. A rubric for being responsive to diversity was developed by Pamela Hays, PhD. In 2007, she published the ADDRESSING model:

A = Age and Generation

D = Developmental Disabilities

D = Acquired Disabilities

R = Religion and Spirituality

E = Ethnicity

S = Socioeconomic Status

S = Sexual Orientation

I = Indigenous Heritage

N = National Origin

G = Gender

This may not be a comprehensive rubric for diversity, but it is considerably more inclusive than focusing on race and ethnicity alone. Diversity is a dynamic component of clients' and clinicians' lives. Many of the factors in the ADDRESSING model interact with one another and may also change over time. However, this rubric provides a starting point for discussion and consideration throughout treatment. Having similarities and differences between client and clinician does not inherently mean a clinician is competent or incompetent to treat a particular client. Rather it provides information to be considered and investigated with the client before drawing any conclusions, and helps the clinician identify areas where particular care may need to be taken.

In many cases, it would be considered inappropriate to provide treatment to minority-culture individuals with exclusively dominant-culture models. EBPs may not be appropriate for a diverse clientele that includes people of color, varying religious and spiritual or socioeconomic backgrounds, sexual orientations, indigenous heritages and ages or generations. All professional organizations hold clinicians accountable to treat every individual with care, respect, courtesy and competency. The competing demands arising from using EBPs and providing culturally-responsive services represents another area where clinicians must work to develop a dialectical balance.

While a comprehensive discussion of diversity is beyond the scope of this text, we strongly encourage clinicians to continually update their knowledge of cultural competency and the interaction with EBPs.

Remaining relationship-oriented while completing paperwork and insurance reviews

A strength of many clinicians is that they are relationship-oriented. They are able to build safe and intimate relationships with a variety of children, teenagers, adults and older adults. While the research supports the use of EBPs, it also supports the importance of the therapeutic relationship; and many clinicians would agree that the relationship is a critical factor in the success of therapy or treatment.

Completing paperwork and insurance reviews may be a funding requirement and, therefore, part of a clinician's job. Other times, there may be laws, regulations, risk-management protocols and standards of care requiring all treatment be documented. Unfortunately, paperwork takes time away from clinical services and may present a barrier to a strong therapeutic alliance because of the time and energy it requires and the frustration it sometimes causes. At the same time, viewing paperwork as an unnecessary evil to be avoided will only facilitate the negative behavior of failing to complete documentation adequately.

Clinicians can balance these opposing needs by maintaining the dialectical mindset that both the relationship and the paperwork are part of the clinical process. Viewing paperwork as clinical documentation, and also learning to effectively manage time and reduce procrastination, are aspects that will help produce balance. Clinicians will benefit from taking some time each day, when possible, to complete documentation and to make it a useful and accurate record of the treatment being provided. Individualized documentation may take more effort to create, but in the end, it will be more useful to the clinician, supervisor, insurance company, client, family members and other members of the treatment team. It is recommended that clinicians create documentation standards and forms to reduce redundancy, and utilize technology to support a streamlined and efficient documentation process.

Encouraging clients to engage in more effective self-care, while maintaining sufficient self-care practices

Establishing effective self-care regimens helps clients manage stress and improve their lives. Some clients come into therapy or treatment with significant impairments in their ability to engage in effective self-care. Educating and assisting these clients in implementing daily self-care is an essential part of the treatment process.

However, some of the same clinicians who make self-care an important goal for their clients engage in ineffective, little, or no self-care themselves. Some clinicians believe they must work as hard as possible, consistently giving more than 100% of themselves to their clients. This may be due to unchecked codependency issues or over-attachment to doing the work. Unfortunately, if clinicians are always helping others, they may burn out and leave the field. Additionally, taking too much care of others fosters dependence, which is the very opposite of empowering clients to take care of themselves. Clinicians will make progress toward a dialectical balance when they can "walk the talk" with the same dedication they encourage their clients to have. All the same things that are helpful for clients are also helpful for clinicians: balanced nutrition, exercise, sleep, hygiene, healthy support systems, etc.

Furthermore, because human services work is challenging and, at times, exhausting, having stress management skills, a sense of humor, a long-term perspective and the ability to have fun in the workplace are essential. Self-care is an ethical obligation of clinicians and clinical supervisors; it is in the best interest of the mental health field as a whole for self-care to be part of the process for staff and clinicians.

There are many DBT skills that are useful for self-care in the work environment.

Turtling	Wise Mind	Effectively
Nonjudgmental	Willingness	Half Smile
Turning the Mind	Ride the Wave	Lemonade
MEDDSS	Broken Record	Radical Acceptance
GIVE and FAST	DEAR SELF	

Diagnosing and seeing deficits, and having a strengths-based perspective

There are two competing perspectives regarding mental health that currently dominate the field: one that focuses on deficits and another that focuses on strengths. Many training programs and clinical texts outline symptoms and pathologies, and some mental health and addiction models (such as the medical model) view problems from a deficit, or disease, perspective. In recent years, however, a growing contingent has moved away from the deficit perspective to focus on clients' strengths. The strengths-based approach advocates focusing on healthy development and emphasizing clients' strengths to empower them to deal with difficulties and stressors effectively. Being strengths-based taps into an individual's resiliency and offers an optimistic and hopeful perspective.

Maintaining a balance between each of these perspectives is useful. Many clients have problems that can be solved, deficits that can be overcome, skills that can be expanded and strengths that can be improved for the client's own benefit. Considering both sides often results in an increase in functioning, relationship effectiveness, and life satisfaction. Holding this dialectical balance helps clinicians and clients acknowledge that there are strengths and weaknesses in each person; and learning to minimize weaknesses and optimize strengths fosters dialectical thinking and behavior.

Wanting clients to change, while not always being patient or positively reinforcing change

Clinicians believe in change; therapy and treatment are all about improving the client's life. Clients may also want things to change, whether that change is in themselves, in others, or in the world around them. Unfortunately, both clinicians and clients may expect a significant change to happen quickly and to be long-lasting; when in reality, change often does not happen quickly, and there is potential for a return to old behaviors once the change has occurred. Clinicians, clients and their families may become impatient and have unrealistic expectations, or differing opinions, about how, when, and even who will change. However, during this process it is important for clinicians to provide clients with encouragement, coaching and rewards for any movement toward positive change. Failing to provide reinforcement can result in clients making little or no change.

The Transtheoretical Model, or SOC, provides an important framework for understanding where the client is in the change process, since intervention recommendations differ (Prochaska, Norcross, & DiClemente, 1994) depending on the client's SOC on a particular issue. Change is not always a linear, straightforward process. Utilizing the SOC framework can help clients build motivation for change and empower them to sustain the change over time. (For additional suggestions about how to foster change, see *Motivational Interviewing* by William Miller & Stephen Rollnick, 2012.)

Clinicians can achieve dialectical balance in expecting change by being patient and positively reinforcing efforts to change. To do so, clinicians can utilize shaping principles or the SOC framework, and assist clients in increasing their internal motivation for change (Prochaska & Prochaska, 2016). The Decisional Balance intervention can be particularly helpful in moving the client forward (Miller & Rollnick, 2012).

Are clients ready for change?

The Pros & Cons worksheet on the next page can aid the clinician in helping the client examine if they are ready to change, and thereby ready to enter into DBT treatment, or not. Pros & Cons looks at one option (usually doing something or changing) and the alternative option (typically not doing something or staying the same).

For clients who find numbers more helpful than words, adding a rating of 0 to 10 for pros, with 10 being the best, and 0 to negative 10 for the cons, with negative 10 being the worst, can be helpful. It allows clients to see quality rather than simply quantity. In the Pros & Cons exercise, work with your client to identify what is good about staying the same, and what isn't so good about it, as well as what is good about changing and what isn't so good about changing.

Pros & Cons

Positives for Staying the Same	Negatives of Changing

Negatives for Staying the Same	Positives of Changing

Stages of Change

Precontemplation	
<u>Definition:</u>
Not being aware of the problem. Doesn't think change is necessary. Wants things to stay the same.	<u>Suggested Interventions:</u>
• *Focus on Motivational Interviewing techniques*
• *Identify DBT skills the clients are using without realizing it*
Contemplation	
<u>Definition:</u>
Considering options. Open to the idea of change, but is hoping not much effort will be required. Not ready to make any changes yet.	<u>Suggested Interventions:</u>
• *Square Breathing*
• *Turning the Mind*
• *Feeling Not Acting*
• *CARES*
• *Relationship Assumptions*
Preparation	
<u>Definition:</u>
Has decided to change. Making plans. Can go too slowly or too quickly through this stage.	<u>Suggested Interventions:</u>
• *ONE MIND*
• *Self-Soothe Kit*
• *Lemonade*
• *Ride the Wave*
Action	
<u>Definition:</u>
Putting the plan into action. Making changes.	<u>Suggested Interventions:</u>
• *Be Mindful*
• *Radical Acceptance*
• *Opposite to Emotion*
• *GIVE and FAST*

Maintenance	
Definition:	Suggested Interventions:
Changes have taken hold. Has stabilized with a new lifestyle.	• *Turtling* • *Effectively* • *Radical Acceptance* • *MEDDSS* • *Repairs* • *4 Horsemen of the Apocalypse*

Return to Old Behavior/Relapse	
Definition:	Suggested Interventions:
Return to old thinking, feeling, impulses and behavior can happen at any stage. Relapse often starts days or weeks before the actual behavior occurs.	• *Wise Mind* • *Nonjudgmental* • *Crisis Survival Network* • *Half Smile* • *BEHAVIORS* • *DEAR SELF*

Being critical of self, while being compassionate toward others

Much has been written about the importance of compassion and empathy in the therapeutic process and how they facilitate change in clients, and these are qualities that many models of therapy require of clinicians. Some clients display problematic social skills or engage in destructive behaviors. Having an understanding, compassionate stance with these clients welcomes them to the therapeutic process so the work can proceed and change can occur.

Unfortunately, the same clinicians who are able to form these supportive therapeutic alliances with clients may have very little compassion toward themselves. These clinicians may be critical of their abilities and highlight their weaknesses. They may hold themselves to higher standards of competence or productivity than they hold clients or colleagues to, and when they don't meet these standards, they judge themselves negatively. They may tap into thoughts about being incompetent, a fraud or impostor, or lacking clinical talent. The more they believe they lack competency, the more evidence they can find to support their perspective, while at the same time ignoring any data that contradicts it. This self-fulfilling prophecy creates self-doubt and distress.

Balance can be achieved with this dialectic by ensuring that compassion for clients doesn't become enabling, while at the same time appreciating one's own strengths and suspending the need to be so self-critical.

Being committed to professional endeavors and investing in personal life

Similar to the self-care dialectic, clinicians may find themselves out of balance and struggling to have both a full personal life and an engaging professional career. Being a human services clinician can be a thankless job at times. Unfortunately, there is often an overwhelming need and insufficient funding for many human services. Even private practice clinicians may experience tension around client need and limited financial resources. As a result, many clinicians may find themselves working very hard and putting in a lot of hours that take most, or all, of their energy.

Having the time and energy to engage in personal activities, such as family and friendships, religious or spiritual practices, and hobbies or other recreational pursuits, can be a struggle for the clinician with a full professional life, as professional obligations tend to outweigh the investment in one's personal life. Clinicians may find themselves devoting 90–100% of their focus to their professional activities and practically none to their personal lives. This imbalance can lead to frustration, exhaustion and burnout— which can cause clinicians to leave the human services field completely. Therefore, it is important that clinicians find an adequate balance between their personal and professional needs.

Clinicians can find a dialectical balance by having functional boundaries with professional endeavors, developing the ability to leave work at work, and not enabling clients or peers by over-caretaking. Enacting these boundaries ensures clinicians have the time and energy to participate fully in their own personal lives.

Being competent while having a lifelong commitment to learning

The ethical guidelines for nearly all human services professionals require clinicians to be competent in their professional endeavors, including the populations they treat and the particular models or interventions they use. The original licensure and certification processes are designed to document demonstration of competence in providing clinical services. These same professional organizations and licensing boards also charge clinicians to engage in lifelong learning through continuing education classes, home-study courses, professional conferences, immersion experiences, clinical supervision, etc.

Balance is found when clinicians can establish a minimum competency in the work while engaging in ongoing professional development and maintaining a commitment to using state-of-the-art models and interventions appropriate to the client populations they serve.

Wanting to be good at DBT before being ready to invest the time and energy to do so

Although it is possible to start using some DBT skills right after taking a seminar or reading about it, building competency with DBT takes time, energy and dedication. Individuals truly interested in implementing DBT in a comprehensive way will need to read about the model, practice it in their own lives, engage in professional consultation and supervision and perhaps even invest in an immersion training experience. Because there is so much to this model, it is possible to spend months, or even a few years, integrating DBT into one's clinical practice.

Like clients, clinicians experience a variety of paradoxes in their professional endeavors, and they, too, will benefit from being able to achieve a dialectical balance in these areas. This will help build resilience in their work lives, improve their effectiveness, and create credibility with clients by "walking the talk." Gaining insight into the experiences of being in and out of balance can also show the clinician some of the challenges and opportunities that clients face as part of balancing dialectics.

THERAPEUTIC ALLIANCE DIALECTICS

The following dialectics are dynamic interactions between the client, the clinician, and the treatment system, which warrant attention in the therapeutic process:

- Acceptance and change
- Centeredness and flexibility
- Nurturing and benevolently demanding
- Emotional intimacy and boundaries
- Unconditional positive regard with limits and natural and logical consequences
- Skill enhancement and self-acceptance
- Problem-solving vs. problem acceptance
- Self-efficacy and asking for help
- Irreverent and validating communication
- Immediate needs, short-term goals and long-term outcomes

Acceptance and change

The dialectic between acceptance and change is a major underlying tenant of DBT. On the one hand, acceptance of the client and their situation, the clinician and the system is useful. This is a place to have understanding and compassion for the client, oneself and the community. This idea of acceptance can be seen in the DBT philosophy that clients are doing the best they can, given their internal strengths and weaknesses and their environmental experiences.

Clients' thoughts and behaviors are a result of what they have learned about themselves, others and the world around them. For example, when life is threatening and unsafe, it makes sense that clients engage in significant controlling behavior; or when life is very hard most, or all, of the time, being suicidal makes logical sense to the clients experiencing such difficulties. Clinicians should also be accepting of their own strengths and weaknesses, and their own learning history. Additionally, although there are certainly many imperfections in most local and national treatment systems, there are also areas of resilience and strength overall.

However, the other half of this dialectic is that change is required. Many times, the only valid option for clients is to work hard, learn DBT skills and change. Although change is often a difficult process that takes hard work, dedication, frustration tolerance and the ability to make mistakes and stay the course, change also empowers clients to experience improvement, hope and optimism. Furthermore, sometimes the best learning comes from negative experiences and disappointments.

DBT requires a balance of acceptance and expecting change. Helping the client find this balance can be facilitated by the clinician providing support and normalizing the client's experiences, while also engaging the client in well-timed interventions designed to move them forward. Using the SOC framework will assist in this process.

Centeredness and flexibility

Centeredness is being grounded in the midst of the pain and trauma the client has experienced, whether from childhood, adulthood or both. The therapy process may entail bearing witness to this pain and trauma, and the clinician's ability to make therapy safe and supportive will facilitate this process. Clinicians need to be able to sit with clients as they explore their experiences, losses, grief and disappointments, and the client finds the strength to be effective in their lives in the here-and-now. This ability to stay present in the face of enormous pain and emotional intensity is an important clinical competency.

Centeredness is also having appropriate boundaries, including emotional, physical, financial, and interpersonal boundaries. It is important for clinicians to set and hold appropriate boundaries, as clients will increase their effectiveness when they work within such boundaries. While some boundaries can be flexible, being too flexible by not enforcing the rules may allow the client to continue in their nonproductive behavior.

Flexibility is about meeting clients where they are and focusing on what they want to work on. Flexibility may be about setting aside the agenda for one session or letting the client "off the hook" from practicing the skills on occasion.

Being out of balance with flexibility or centeredness can look like being rigid or too loose. The challenge is to do a little bit of both without doing too much of either. Achieving a dialectical balance between centeredness and flexibility can be accomplished by staying in the moment, holding the boundaries and bending and flexing therapeutically when appropriate.

Nurturing and benevolently demanding

Nurturing is being a coach, teacher or mentor to the client. Here the clinician provides positive reinforcement for anything that supports the client in staying the course with therapy and integrating DBT skills into their lives. Nurturing provides support and understanding for the client when they are frustrated, experiencing a setback or feeling like a failure.

Benevolently demanding is part of effective parenting and is the basis of the educational system. It is about having high and achievable expectations. Goals and expectations should be set high enough so clients need to stretch and grow, while not being so hard that clients become frustrated and give up nor so easy that clients become bored and lose interest. Having supportive and challenging expectations fosters development. Clients may grow and improve in ways they may not have imagined possible. Setting high and achievable goals also shows the client the clinician believes in them, and it may even provide an opportunity for the client to experience surprise about how much they can actually achieve when they commit to putting in the effort. This experience can be incredibly motivating, validating and empowering for clients.

This dialectic is about working hard and giving the client credit for the work they have accomplished, but also being flexible at times by taking a break or slowing down. Balance can be achieved when clinicians provide positive reinforcement for progress made, while pushing the client forward to live in more effective ways.

Emotional intimacy and boundaries

Therapy is an emotionally intimate experience in many cases, which often draws the client and the clinician closer together. Depending on the therapy model, learning about emotions, working through the pain and learning not to act on emotions are part of the therapeutic process. Clients are exposing their vulnerabilities, sharing their deepest fears and grappling with their own imperfections. The safety and groundedness that clinicians provide allows the client to go even deeper emotionally on a regular basis. As clients explore their internal realities and environmental experiences, they may have a wide range of emotions in the therapy room: from despair to anger, and even tears. In the midst of these emotional expressions, the therapeutic relationship is intensified, and clinicians may experience increased attachment and appreciation for the client.

While this work is emotionally intimate, it is still important to maintain boundaries. Therapy is not an interaction of peers. Clients are seeking help, whether they come voluntarily or are mandated to treatment. They share their understanding of their life, struggles and painful experiences, and replicate their relationships in the therapy room. The clinician, however, is in this relationship as a professional. The clinician is there to be a guide and mentor, not to share their own struggles and painful experiences. As the relationship becomes deeper and more intimate, clients and clinicians may drift into looser boundaries. This is a slippery slope that can lead to confusion, boundary crossings and, in its extreme forms, inappropriate behavior.

It is the clinician's responsibility to find dialectical balance here. The clinician can do so by meeting their own needs outside of the therapy room, using supervision and consultation, knowing when they need their own therapy and having a thorough informed consent process.

Informed consent outlines what happens in therapy and what doesn't. While this is a written contract created at the beginning of therapy, it can also be an ongoing understanding of what is appropriate in therapy and what isn't. Clients haven't always grown up in functional families with healthy boundaries, so it makes sense they will push and resist limits set by the clinician. As the professional, it is the clinician's responsibility to maintain boundaries while not becoming unnecessarily rigid.

Unconditional positive regard with limits and natural and logical consequences

Unconditional positive regard, in which the clinician forms an empathic relationship with the client, is a major component of humanistic psychology. The clinician accepts the client for who they are, rather than defining them based on their behavior. Part of this therapeutic process involves being nonjudgmental with clients. It is about not assigning a value to the client as good or bad, even though their behavior may have positive or negative connotations.

Behavior provokes natural and logical consequences that can be positive or negative. Clients completing homework and demonstrating DBT skills in their lives should receive the natural and logical consequences of praise, encouragement and the expectation to learn additional skills. When a client doesn't practice skills, the natural and logical consequences could be role-playing the skill in session, discussing why the skill was not practiced, and letting the client know the expectation is to practice the skill outside of therapy. Not showing up or derailing the therapy may require setting expectations for therapy, holding the client accountable and perhaps even behavioral contracts. When the behavior is extreme—such as acting out in the office, being threatening or destroying property—terminating the therapy relationship may be the most appropriate action.

However, there is a fine line between natural and logical consequences, and punishment—which is defined by the level of severity and whether there is a component of acting out negative feelings on the part of the clinician. This can happen when the clinician's countertransference goes unchecked, and their reactions become an expression of frustration, irritation and anger at the client. The other extreme is not applying natural and logical consequences when they are appropriate and warranted due to over-identification with the client or their circumstances.

Achieving a dialectical balance in this area requires forming relationships with clients without enabling them, and applying natural and logical consequences in a consistent manner. Clinicians are also encouraged to keep their codependency in check and see both the positives and negatives in the therapeutic relationship, in the client's behaviors and in their own behaviors.

Skill enhancement and self-acceptance

Some clients are interested in increasing their skills, and they spend a lot of time and energy in this pursuit. They have read many self-help books, spend hours on the internet and watch media clinicians like Dr. Phil. They listen to advice and watch for new trends in life, career and family perspectives. These clients believe their problems will be solved when they find the next great idea, way of life or spiritual or philosophical perspective. They are constantly searching to find the solution outside themselves. While in this pursuit, however, they don't give themselves credit for the strengths and skills they do have; and they don't maintain awareness of the ways in which they have grown and improved their lives.

There are other clients who are all about self-acceptance. They believe they are fine and don't need to change in any way. If a change needs to happen, it must be about other people. These clients have personal philosophies that sound like, "It's my way or the highway," "You're either with me or against me" or "Love me or leave me alone." Unfortunately, there is error in logic with this position. There is always something new to learn or to improve. For many clients, there may be considerable room for improvement, even among those who are functioning adequately. In addition to this logic being erroneous, it may also be arrogant. Clients with this perspective may be disrespectful, aggressive and perhaps even ignore the rights of others.

Either of these two perspectives can benefit from a little of the other to achieve balance. Clinicians can assist each of these client perspectives by helping them see that a little more acceptance, or enhancement of their skills, will be useful. Striking a dialectical balance involves helping clients become aware that they can improve and increase their skills, while also learning to accept themselves and their lives. Doing so will empower clients to be more effective so that they can build a life worth living.

Problem-solving vs. problem acceptance

There are times when problems can be solved. Clients can figure out solutions by asking family, friends and clinicians for advice or ideas, using their past experiences, or researching what to do on the internet or at the library; they can advocate for themselves, act to solve the problem and be curious about trying other things if the first thing they try doesn't work. This can be a very effective process; and yet, there are also problems that can't be solved.

When a problem can't be solved or resolved in a satisfactory manner, accepting the problem may make sense. Sometimes clients learn they don't always get it their way no matter how hard they work, how much they ask for help or how much they apologize. A client accepting there are things they cannot control is an important step in being empowered to invest where they do have control. Clients can also be out of balance with this part of the dialectic when they sink into passivity. They may think nearly everything is out of their control, and taking a victim or martyr stance may be a natural part of this imbalance. However, clients can still maintain control over their thoughts, feelings and behavior even when problems can't be solved.

A variation of this dialectic is regulating and tolerating emotions. Clients have many opportunities to learn to cope with, manage and regulate their emotions; indeed, this may be an everyday occurrence. By comparison, there are times when the only thing that can be done is to tolerate emotions. This may be true with strong emotions and those that last a long time, such as grief. There may be no way to resolve the loss the client is grieving, and perhaps all they can do is tolerate and accept the grief for a while. However, it is also possible for a client to get stuck in grief and stay in it too long. In these situations, the client will eventually need to move away from the grief and into living life in the here-and-now, with the loss as part of their history.

Clinicians can help clients find balance between problem-solving and problem acceptance by alternating active strategies with acceptance perspectives.

Self-efficacy and asking for help

Some clients live their lives as if they can do everything themselves. They may have learned not to trust others. Family and friends may have disappointed them in the past when they didn't help or made things worse than they needed to be. Having learned to be self-contained because others aren't reliable, these clients attempt to be their only resource. There are probably many things for which clients can rely on themselves as their self-efficacy increases; however, there is a limit to what any one person can do on their own. Clinicians may encounter this situation when a client won't talk about what is difficult or challenging and won't take suggestions or direction.

At the other extreme are clients who ask for help even when they can do things themselves. These clients become dependent on others when they don't need to be. They look for others to give direction and solve their problems even when they have the skills and resources to take care of themselves in many ways. Clinicians see evidence of this imbalance when the client can't seem to make decisions, requires concrete directions from the clinician, seeks regular approval for their choices or actions, or makes excessive requests for help on basic issues.

Clinicians can help clients work toward striking a dialectical balance in this area by helping them acknowledge that life isn't about being entirely codependent or entirely independent. Clients can effectively take care of themselves and manage their lives while also knowing when, how and whom to ask for help.

Irreverent and validating communication

Irreverent communication is about having fun, displaying a sense of humor, and not taking oneself too seriously. Therapists can poke fun at themselves to model to clients that it is ok to laugh at themselves and not always be so intense. Irreverent communication also seeks to disrupt crisis-building behavior. It responds to the most outrageous or worrisome part of what the client is saying and takes it a step farther, illustrating the client's position is extreme and perhaps illogical. Having fun and a sense of humor in therapy can be helpful, and yet it can also be disrespectful or passive-aggressive if not handled appropriately. It is crucial that the clinician use this communication style with skill and confidence.

By comparison, validating communication is supportive. It acknowledges the reality of the client's life. Many clients grow up hearing that their thoughts, feelings, and behaviors are wrong, inaccurate, and unacceptable, and they live in environments and participate in relationships that invalidate them and teach them that they should be different from who they are.

Therapy and treatment should validate the client, with the clinician accepting the reality of the client's life while also helping them to see other perspectives. Clinicians can achieve balance in the therapeutic relationship with this dialectic by ensuring each session has a good amount of both irreverent and validating communication. This communication should be a two-way street with both the clinician and client participating in this communication process.

Immediate needs, short-term goals and long-term outcomes

This is a three-way dialectic wherein the client, clinician and therapy balance immediate needs, short-term goals and long-term outcomes. Attention and effort need to be made periodically in each domain. Being unable to strike a dialectical balance here can lead to progress being made in one of these areas, but at the cost of other areas.

Clinicians can help achieve balance with this dialectic by empowering clients to meet their immediate needs while working toward their short-term goals, as well as keeping an eye on their ultimate desired outcome. All the preceding therapeutic alliance dialectics can contribute to finding a successful dialectical balance in these areas.

Being out of balance in one or more of these dialectical areas can cause the therapy to lose forward momentum. It is the responsibility of the clinician to maintain balance in the therapeutic relationship and to make adjustments as needed.

DIALECTIC CONCLUSIONS

There are many opportunities for balance and imbalance for the client, the clinician and in the interactions between clients and clinicians. Balance can be experienced internally or in the context of interactions, and it facilitates the clinical work and fosters the relationship for the benefit of both individuals.

However, balance is imperfect. It doesn't have to be exactly in the center. It is possible to be in balance while still being a bit askew. It is also possible to vacillate between one side and the other, while still being in balance. The previous lists are only a sampling of the dialectics that might be present for the client, clinician or in the therapeutic relationship. Some questions clinicians might ask themselves to help foster a dialectical stance are on the following worksheet.

Identifying and Addressing Dialectics
— Clinician Worksheet —

This worksheet is intended to help you generate ideas about client and clinician dialectics and how to manage them as effectively as you can. Answer the questions below and feel free to examine additional areas where dialectics might be present beyond those listed.

1. What additional dialectics would improve client experiences?

    _____

    _____

    _____

2. How can clients achieve a dialectical balance?

    _____

    _____

    _____

3. What dialectics do clinicians experience in their work?

    _____

    _____

    _____

4. How can clinicians achieve a dialectical balance?

    _____

    _____

    _____

5. What dialectics are present in the therapeutic relationship?

    _____

    _____

    _____

6. How can the therapeutic relationship achieve a dialectical balance?

    _____

    _____

    _____

Chapter 3

The Skills Modules: Individual Skills, Diary Cards, Chain Analysis and Treatment Plans

DBT consists of four content areas: Mindfulness, Distress Tolerance, Emotion Regulation, and Interpersonal Effectiveness.

MINDFULNESS

Mindfulness is about voluntarily, intentionally paying attention to the current moment in a nonjudgmental fashion. It is also about maintaining an awareness of internal experiences such as sensations, energy levels, thoughts, emotions and impulses, as well as external experiences of what's going on in the environment and with interactions. It is staying present in the moment on both the inside and the outside to minimize interpretations, assumptions, abstractions and judgments. This focus on the here-and-now can be found in many models, such as Gestalt Therapy, third-wave CBT models, Western religions and Eastern spiritual practices.

By being grounded in the here-and-now, clients are able to respond to what is going on, both on the inside and the outside. They are empowered to act in their own best interests.

In DBT, mindfulness is also about balance—balancing emotions, thoughts, behaviors and relationships in the here-and-now, as well as balancing the present with the past and the future. Some clients spend a considerable amount of time in the past. They may ruminate, analyze and find themselves "less-than." For other clients, the future is all-consuming. These clients catastrophize, worry about what will happen and criticize themselves for not having other options. Then there is a third group of clients who spend a majority of their time in both the past and the future. For these clients, there may be a strong sense that life is passing them by—which may be an accurate perception since they do not spend a significant amount of time in the here-and-now.

Although mindfulness emphasizes spending the most time in the present moment, it does allow for a focus on the past or the future. Staying connected to the past and the future can be productive when done in a mindful and intentional manner, rather than in ways that are distracting, intrusive, overwhelming and distressing. Clients can reflect upon, learn from and make sense of the past. Similarly, clients can also plan, prepare for and invest in the future. When done, the client returns to the here-and-now.

Nonjudgmental

With DBT's mindfulness skills, clients learn to be nonjudgmental, which involves not assigning a value to yourself or others. Individuals are not good or bad. Many individuals often judge themselves as unlovable, damaged, evil or imperfect, while they may also judge others as worthwhile, superior, and perfect. Or they may hold themselves to higher standards than they hold others to—standards that are often unachievable for the average person, which is a setup for failure and negative self-judgment. Furthermore, being judgmental drives problematic, destructive behavior. If the client is unworthy or evil, shouldn't they be unhappy and in pain? This faulty logic justifies engaging in behavior that makes their lives worse and more painful. These clients can then judge their dysfunctional lives as confirmation of being unlovable, damaged and unworthy. This circular thinking perpetuates a self-fulfilling prophecy.

Although positive judgments may seem acceptable, they are also problematic. Placing a value on oneself or others as good, deserving or perfect is a slippery slope—as it implies that there are others who are bad, undeserving and imperfect. Positive judgments can easily lead to negative judgments, which can foster arrogance and looking down on others. Positive judgments can also feel inaccurate or false, causing clients to judge themselves as impostors and frauds.

In addition, although clients can learn to be nonjudgmental with themselves and others, they can't stop other people from judging them. Clients will benefit from developing the ability to let others' judgments roll off them, rather than letting them "stick" and take hold in their self-image. It will also be effective if clients can avoid judging others who are judging them.

It is important to note that being nonjudgmental is an ideal to strive for. It is not a concrete achievement that can be accomplished one day and then it is done for the foreseeable future. It is something to be worked on every day. There are days when clients will be more effective with being nonjudgmental and other days they will be less so. However, it is important that when clients find themselves judging, they identify the judgments, show compassion toward themselves, and recommit to being as nonjudgmental as possible.

An individual's behavior doesn't indicate anything about the value of the individual, although the behavior may be helpful, problematic, healthy, destructive or inappropriate. One of the goals of therapy is to help clients move away from this behavior toward life-enhancing behaviors. It is crucial to figure out what purpose the problematic, destructive behavior serves. When the purpose is to confirm their judgments, DBT teaches clients to be nonjudgmental with themselves and others. Other needs include modulating pain, providing intensity, feeling alive and getting support from others. DBT helps the client learn to replace their problematic, self-destructive behaviors with DBT skills that will meet these needs without the costs or damages caused by current strategies. The skills contained in the Mindfulness, Distress Tolerance, Emotion Regulation and Interpersonal Effectiveness modules can provide the tools necessary to be successful in being nonjudgmental.

DISTRESS TOLERANCE

The traditional DBT framework sequences the Distress Tolerance module as the third module because it is a subgroup of skills under the Emotion Regulation umbrella. However, teaching these skills sooner rather than later meets the clients where they are and provides them the opportunity for relief in the early stages of treatment.

Crises and distress are the issues that typically bring individuals and families into therapy. Clients and their families want assistance with, as well as solutions to, the problems they are experiencing. The skills contained in this module provide them with tools to cope with, manage, distract from and tolerate crises, stress and chaos. If they experience some relief or find some solutions early in the process, this increases engagement, compliance with homework assignments and the odds of staying in therapy when it becomes more challenging.

Some frustrations can be tolerated, while others can be modulated. Distress Tolerance is about frustration tolerance, which involves the ability to manage frustration and stress without engaging in negative, problematic or destructive behaviors. Increased generalization of frustration tolerance occurs as childhood progresses. However, adult clients who have experienced disrupted development because of abuse, trauma or other intervening factors, may still be attempting to complete this milestone successfully.

Part of frustration tolerance is moving away from willfulness. Willfulness is a mindset clients may have: they want it their way just because they do. Willfulness is also about the feelings and behaviors that go along with the mindset of "my way or the highway." Sometimes clients want what they want without any solid reasoning behind their desire. Because willfulness is fleeting, when the client gets what they want it doesn't last long enough, so then the client has to want something else. Unfortunately, willfulness usually comes with a cost to energy levels, relationships and quality of life; and it tells clients that when they don't get what they want they are failures.

By comparison, Distress Tolerance encourages clients to be willing. Willingness involves the ability to tolerate hearing "no" or being disappointed, as well as doing what works in a given situation and behaving in a manner that is effective. Willingness teaches clients that sometimes they get their way, sometimes others get it their way and whenever possible, it is optimal for both to get their way. (Sometimes the client not getting what they want is the most useful lesson and can lead to an unexpected outcome.) Willingness is about collaboration, trusting the process, letting go of control, and not sweating the small stuff. It is energy-generating, fosters relationships and increases quality of life.

EMOTION REGULATION

In this module, clients learn about their emotions, achieve a deeper understanding of their emotional life, and develop greater resiliency when dealing with emotions. Although emotions are part of life, sometimes clients believe they shouldn't have any emotions, or they should only have positive emotions. Therefore, when they have negative emotions such as anger, sadness or loneliness, they may feel they need to get rid of them. They may also judge themselves by the emotions they experience.

Two major components of this module are assisting clients in learning impulse control and to delay gratification. Part of this process is having clients realize that they can feel an impulse or strong emotion without acting on it. Instead, they can learn to tolerate the impulse or emotion, which is exemplified in the skill *Riding the Wave*. By *Riding the Wave*, they are harnessing the energy, impulse or emotion, staying mindfully present with it, and being patient until it shifts into the next impulse or emotion in the same way waves rise and fall. In addition to *Riding the Wave*, clients can choose to use a DBT skill to deal with the impulse, they can choose to act on the impulse or emotion in a less harmful way, or they can choose to act on the impulse at full strength. In this last option, they are actively choosing to engage with it instead of feeling as if it is happening on autopilot or as if they are merely reacting to it.

Emotion Regulation also requires the ability to recognize when an emotional experience is occurring. Unfortunately, many people have difficulty identifying and even naming different emotions. Without an understanding of the emotions being experienced, it can be difficult for a client to identify appropriate and healthy strategies for managing those emotions. For that reason, some clients may need some psychoeducation to be better prepared to name, and cope with, emotions. This ability to identify and understand emotions can also be incredibly useful in navigating personal relationships and challenging situations in a variety of settings.

INTERPERSONAL EFFECTIVENESS

According to DBT, there are three types of interpersonal effectiveness: Objective, Relationship, and Self-Respect Effectiveness. Objective effectiveness is about clients accomplishing some objective, whether that is getting what they want in relationships, meeting a need or having their opinion heard. Clients learn how to ask for what they want and how to tolerate not always getting what they want. Relationship effectiveness is about building healthy, respectful, and responsive relationships. Self-respect effectiveness is about knowing oneself, being assertive, setting boundaries, valuing oneself, and not putting others' needs first.

Interestingly, relationship and self-respect effectiveness form a dialectic: balancing self and others, giving and receiving, and learning healthy codependence. The skills in this module teach clients how to have functional relationships by helping clients balance their needs with the needs of others. This empowers them to communicate in clear and respectful ways, and helps them deal with difficult or challenging people with whom they interact.

DBT SKILLS

The skills in this text are organized into three categories:

- Meta Skills: The most important and perhaps the biggest DBT skill set.

- Secondary Skills: Additional skills individuals find helpful after learning and using Meta Skills.

- Ancillary Skills: Skills that may be particularly useful for a unique client or specific situation.

On the following pages are a variety of DBT skills that fall within the Mindfulness, Distress Tolerance, Emotion Regulation and Interpersonal Effectiveness modules. However, these are not the only skills that can be used when teaching clients. Clinicians can also find additional skills in other texts, on the internet and in professional articles; or they can create their own skills using the following framework:

- Determine for which module you are developing the skills

- Take into consideration cultural values, developmental milestones and clients' worldviews

- Outline how the skill will facilitate balanced dialectics

- Make it relevant to your clients

- Appeal to visual, auditory and kinesthetic learners

- Be responsive to your clients' attention spans

- Utilize multiple forms of media

- Make learning fun, interesting, creative and relevant

- Learn from the wisdom of your clients

Meta Skills

Mindfulness	
Effectively	• Working to be as effective as we can in our lives. Doing what works in a given situation. • Identifying what is more effective, and avoiding less effective strategies and behaviors in our lives. • Avoiding judgmental words such as better, worse, good or bad.
Non judgmental	• Suspending evaluations about self and others. • Acknowledging behavior as harmful or helpful, but not judging it as right or wrong, good or bad. This also means not judging the person engaging in the behavior. Behavior can generate natural consequences, but we don't label the person. • Describing things concretely, in *Nonjudgmental* terms. • Liking or disliking things, while not judging ourselves or others. • Holding values that are beliefs or ethics, not judgments.
Wise Mind	• Balancing Rational Mind and Emotional Mind to create *Wise Mind*. • We are able to be mindful and effective when we can have both Rational Mind (thoughts) and Emotional Mind (feelings) present in our experiences. Be sure not to judge Rational Mind as "good" and Emotional Mind as "bad." Neither is good nor bad, they are just part of our experiences in life. • By being in *Wise Mind*, we are in balance and have all our senses, ways of knowing and skills at our disposal to manage our lives effectively and to act in our best interest.

Distress Tolerance	
Radical Acceptance	• Example: the Serenity Prayer. • We have the ability to control our thoughts, feelings and actions. • We may have limited control over what happens around us and what others do. • We can effectively focus our attention and energy on what we can control and change: ourselves.

Emotion Regulation						
MEDDSS	**M**astery	**E**xercise	**D**iet	**D**rugs (prescription)	**S**leep	**S**pirituality

Interpersonal Effectiveness				
DEAR SELF	**D**escribe what I want	Be **E**ncouraging	**A**sk for what is wanted	**R**einforce others
	Sometimes tolerate not getting my way	**E**xperiencing the present moment mindfully, inside and outside my body	**L**isten skillfully to myself and others	**F**ind negotiation opportunities
FAST	Be **F**air to myself	**A**pologize less	**S**tick to my values	Be **T**ruthful with myself
GIVE	Be **G**entle	**I**nterested	**V**alidating	Have an **E**asy manner

Secondary Skills

Mindfulness	
Be Mindful	Be mindful of using my skills, engaging in self-care, having healthy fun and connecting to my support system.
Moment to Pause	Take a quick moment to check in with myself on the inside, outside and in my interactions.
Turtling	Take care of myself like a turtle. Retreat inside for safety sometimes, go slowly and methodically, protect myself but don't be aggressive, be adaptive in a variety of situations, use my hard outer shell to let others' judgments roll off my back and get myself back in balance persistently.
Distress Tolerance	
Crisis Survival Network	Create a list of people who support me and use it flexibly.
Half Smile	Find something in my day or life that I can have a genuine *Half Smile* about.
Self-Soothe Kit	Create a kit that is self-soothing and use it when needed.
Emotion Regulation	
Lemonade	Refocusing my weaknesses so they become strengths.
Opposite to Emotion	Engage in the action that will bring the opposite emotion into my awareness to balance the distressing emotion.
Ride the Wave	Imagine I am riding the wave of my emotions and impulses while not acting on them.
Interpersonal Effectiveness	
4 Horsemen of the Apocalypse	Identify the four most destructive things that I bring into my relationships. Be skillful to keep these things out of my relationships.
Broken Record	Be a broken record with myself: keep coming back to my needs.
Repairs	I can apologize, accept apologies and let some things go to be skillful in relationships.

Ancillary Skills

Mindfulness	
Mindful Eating	Focus on eating and chew each bite fully. Notice the complexity of the food, the sensations of fullness and satiation.
Observe, Describe & Participate	Just notice. Become aware of things in this one moment. Describe my experiences in concrete, specific terms that are nonjudgmental. Engage fully and completely in each activity.
ONE MIND	**O**ne thing at a time, be in the **N**ow and grounded in the **E**nvironment. Stay in the **M**oment, **I**ncrease my awareness of my five senses, be **N**onjudgmental and **D**escribe what is going on.
Square Breathing	Breathe in while counting to four. Hold it for four seconds. Then exhale while counting to four. Repeat four times.

Distress Tolerance	
ACCEPTS	Distract myself with **A**ctivities, **C**hoices, **C**ontributions, **E**motions, **P**ushing away, **T**houghts and **S**ensations.
IMPROVE	Distract myself with **I**magery of a beautiful or safe place, find **M**eaning in my life, **P**rayer, **R**elaxation, **O**ne thing at a time, **V**acation from the demands of my life and **E**ncouragement to be effective.
Keeping It In Perspective	Because of everything I have been through, I am able to effectively deal with my life and what is happening to me.
SPECIFIC PATHS	What is my **S**upreme concern? **P**ractice my skills, focus my **E**nergy and **C**oncentration, **I** can be effective, have **F**aith, consider what is **I**mportant, have **C**ourage and **P**atience, pay **A**ttention, complete **T**asks, be **H**umble and have **S**ensitivity.
Turning the Mind	I am in the driver's seat. I can make the choice to drive down an effective path of thinking, feeling and behaving.
Willingness	Practice *Willingness* to accept reality, a bad day, things not going my way or that I can't control others and the world around me.

Ancillary Skills

Emotion Regulation			
ABC	**A**ccumulate positives	**B**uild mastery	**C**ope ahead
BEHAVIOR	Use effective **B**ehavior, be grounded in the **E**nvironment, do things that are **H**ealing not hurting, **A**ct in my best interest, be consistent with my **V**alues, **I**magine getting through difficulties, focus on the desired **O**utcome and **R**einforce my successes.		
CARES	Manage my emotions by being **C**alm, monitoring **A**rousal, finding **R**elaxation and rest, coping with my **E**motions and getting a healthy amount of **S**leep.		
EMOTIONS	**E**xpose myself to emotions, be **M**indful of current emotions, **O**utline a plan to deal with emotions, **T**ake opposite action, **I**ncrease positive experiences, identify **O**bstacles and plan to overcome them, **N**otice what is going on and use my **S**upport system.		
Feeling Not Acting	Use my *Moment to Pause* skill to identify and feel my impulses or urges. I can choose to use a skill to manage it or to tolerate it while doing nothing.		
Love Dandelions	Build an awareness and acceptance of parts of myself I find unattractive or don't like. Manage these things effectively so they don't cause me distress.		

Interpersonal Effectiveness	
Dealing with Difficult People	Be nonjudgmental, participate in improving my relationships, identify and overcome obstacles to improvement.
Relationship Assumptions	This skill puts the dialectical philosophy into the language of couples or families. 1. Both of us are doing the best we can. 2. Both of us can be more effective. 3. Both of us want to be more effective. 4. Both of us have to be more effective, try harder and apply our skills. 5. Neither of us caused all the problems in our relationship, and we both have to work together to solve them.
Relationship Mindfulness	Identify generalizations, describe assumptions, suspend judgments, avoid jumping to conclusions and be empowered in my relationships.
Turn the Tables	Be reciprocal. Do things for other people, without the expectation of getting anything in return.

DIARY CARDS

Another component of DBT involves diary cards, which allow clients to track how often they used their DBT skills each day, including the specific skills they used. By keeping track of, and paying attention to skill use, clients will naturally use more skills more often. In addition to tracking their skills, clients track what problematic urges, emotions and behaviors they are focusing on reducing; they rate the intensity of these, and what skills they used to cope with them. By using diary cards, clients can develop insight into how using their skills results in fewer problematic urges, emotions and behaviors.

Since the publication of Linehan's texts in 1993, many clients and therapists have created variations of diary cards. In recent years, there have been several diary cards and DBT apps created. For more information, search in the app stores on smartphones and tablets.

CHAIN ANALYSIS

Chain analysis is a core DBT tool that is similar to functional analysis. It helps the client identify the links in the chain of events that led them to relapse or to problem behaviors. Clients identify what vulnerabilities may have led to their recent episode, which includes examining the thoughts, feelings, behaviors and urges that encouraged them to act out their problem behaviors. Each of these pieces are called "links" and are conceptualized in terms of being links in the chain of events. After mapping out the chain, the clinician and client discuss which skills might have been used to reduce or eliminate the problem behavior at each link.

Another part of the chain analysis process involves asking what got in the way of using skills at each link and brainstorming how to increase the likelihood that skills will be used in a similar future chain of events. If a client doesn't have a skill that works on a particular link, then it is time to teach new skills. There are many resources available for chain analyses and many formats that can be used. Below is a very simple chain analysis for self-harm impulses on a Friday night:

Chain Analysis	Skills that serve as antidotes to the links
Vulnerabilities link: • Relief experienced with previous self-harm incidents • Interpersonal sensitivity	• *Effectively* • *FAST and DEAR SELF*
Connecting link: • Slept poorly this week • Ate a lot of unhealthy food over the previous two days	• *MEDDSS* • *Mindful Eating*
Triggers link: • Boss expressed dissatisfaction on work performance	• *Wise Mind* • *Nonjudgmental*
Connecting link: • Friends canceled plans to get together Friday night • Feeling lonely, frustrated, and exhausted	• *Crisis Survival Network* • *Self-Soothe Kit*
Problem Behavior: Self-harm	• *Wise Mind* • *Crisis Survival Network*

DBT TREATMENT PLANS AND INTERVENTIONS

Nearly all components of DBT can be placed on treatment plans. Below are a few examples of DBT treatment plans:

Goal: Build a life worth living.

Objectives: Increase a sense of connection and feelings of being understood.

Interventions: Validation will be used to acknowledge that the client's perspective of reality is accurate for them, and that the therapist is developing an understanding of their day-to-day struggles and successes.

Monitoring Progress: Client will demonstrate engagement in therapy by regularly attending sessions. The client will report an increase in feeling connected and being understood by self-report on a 1–10 scale, with 10 representing feeling completely connected and understood.

Goal: Build a life worth living.

Objectives: Increase prosocial behavior while decreasing problematic behavior.

Interventions: Reinforcement will be applied to any discussion of intentions for, or actual, pro-social behavior.

Monitoring Progress: Client's diary card will demonstrate an increase in prosocial behaviors and a decrease in problem behaviors.

Goal: Build a life worth living.

Objectives: To have fewer emotional outbursts so the client experiences less distress and fewer out-of-control feelings.

Interventions: Use the *Wise Mind* skill to reduce emotional outbursts.

Monitoring Progress: Client's diary card will demonstrate a decrease in the number and intensity of emotional outbursts and an increase in the number of times *Wise Mind* was practiced.

Goal: Build a life worth living.

Objectives: Increase a sense of purpose and find meaning in life.

Interventions: Use the *Lemonade* and *Effectively* skills to build on the client's life experiences to find purpose and meaning.

Monitoring Progress: Client will have a greater sense of their values and be on a path to have more purpose in life as evidenced by client self-report in therapy sessions.

Goal: Build a life worth living.

Objectives: Increase interpersonal effectiveness.

Interventions: Use *DEAR SELF* to increase relationship skills and satisfaction.

Monitoring Progress: Diary cards will demonstrate an increase in relationship satisfaction through the use of the *DEAR SELF* skill, which will be tracked.

Goal: Build a life worth living.

Objectives: Increase living in the moment.

Interventions: The client will use mindfulness skills, particularly *Moment to Pause* and *Be Mindful*, to increase being in the here-and-now.

Monitoring Progress: Client's diary card will demonstrate the use of these skills, and contact with the present moment will be evidenced through client's self-report.

Goal: Build a life worth living.

Objectives: Client will learn about their vulnerabilities and triggers and how to use DBT skills to manage them.

Interventions: Use chain analysis to explore how to deal with vulnerabilities and triggers.

Monitoring Progress: Client will track the number of completed chain analyses, demonstrate insight in session weekly, and continue the commitment to use DBT skills to reduce the impact of vulnerabilities and triggers.

SKILLS MODULE TABLES

The following tables have the skills arranged by skills module with a description designed for the clinician rather than the client. These tables can be a handy reference guide when you are new to DBT and are in need of a quick refresher of the skill and its potential benefits for the client.

Mindfulness Skills

Be Mindful	This skill asks clients to be mindful of one or two things. The client pays attention to practicing a specific skill or staying in the moment. Ask clients to *Be Mindful* of self-care, having healthy fun and connecting to their support systems.
Effectively	This skill is about empowering clients to be as effective as possible in their lives. Clients will benefit from seeing what is more effective and avoiding less effective strategies and behaviors. Part of this process includes avoiding judgmental words such as better or worse, good or bad.
Mindful Eating	This exercise is about being fully present in the ritual of eating. It asks clients to experience the complexity and richness of eating. Clients may find themselves eating at their desks at work, in their cars or in front of their TVs. While this may serve a purpose, ask them to find three to four times per week to eat mindfully. Eating mindfully requires that clients focus only on eating. They use their senses to appreciate the food and they chew each bite fully. By doing so, they will eat less food in the 15–20 minutes it takes to feel full. While being mindful, hopefully they will notice the sensation of fullness and satiation. Chewing each bite fully also produces more saliva, which is one of the most effective enzymes in digestion, enabling food to be digested more completely.
Moment to Pause	This skill teaches clients to take a quick moment to check in with themselves on the inside, in their environment and with their interactions. By being grounded inside and around themselves, they are able to make decisions and behave in ways that are in their best interest. By taking a *Moment to Pause*, clients can stop destructive or problematic behaviors and replace them with DBT skills. This is a simple but essential skill in reaching the goal of building a life worth living.
Nonjudgmental	This skill is about reducing distress and negative feelings by suspending evaluations about self and others. This entails judging behavior as right or wrong, good or bad, but not judging or labeling the person engaging in the behavior. Instead of being judgmental, clients can describe things concretely without assigning a value of good or bad. They can maintain their values, opinions and ethics while not judging others who have different values, opinions or ethics.

Mindfulness Skills

Observe, Describe & Participate	Have clients notice what is going on around and inside themselves. Just notice. Become aware of things in this one moment. Have clients put their observations and descriptions of things, situations and people into concrete, specific terms, while being as nonjudgmental as possible. Clients get to have their opinions and values: they can like or dislike something or they can wish something was different. But what they should avoid doing is making judgmental descriptions, which assign a value to themselves or others. For example: "That person is an idiot," "I am terrible and deserve to be in pain" or "It's hopeless, I will never be good enough." By observing what is going on inside and around them and describing things concretely, clients are able to participate mindfully in their lives, and they can partake completely in each activity they engage in.
ONE MIND	This acronym helps clients stay present in the moment inside and around them. **O**ne thing at a time **N**ow: be in the here-and-now **E**nvironment: be grounded in it **M**oment: be present in this one moment **I**ncrease awareness of my five senses to be firmly in the here-and-now **N**onjudgmental of self and others **D**escribe what is going on in concrete, specific terms
Square Breathing	When clients take a few deep breaths, it creates a *Moment to Pause*. Furthermore, it results in increased oxygen to their muscles and brains so they may feel less tense and think more clearly, and it also provides another opportunity for the client to disengage from destructive or problematic behavior and utilize another skill. 1. Breathe in a while counting to four. 2. Hold it for four seconds. 3. Exhale while counting to four. 4. Repeat four times.

Mindfulness Skills

Turtling	Turtles are very important symbols in many cultures or communities, such as Native American and Hindu cultures. Turtling will also resonate with kids and teenagers, because of the Teenage Mutant Ninja Turtles franchise. Clients can use a variety of strategies to take care of themselves, just like turtles: • Retreating inside themselves and then reemerging when it is safe. • Going slowly and methodically; being thoughtful about how to invest time, energy and attention. • Using their hard, outer shells to let things roll off their backs. This is a great way to deflect the judgments of others. • Being adaptive—turtles are able to live in water and on land. • Persistently self-righting. When turtles get turned over, they work hard and use their weight and environment to get themselves right-side up and back in balance. • Although they aren't aggressive animals, turtles will protect themselves when necessary through snapping or biting.
Wise Mind	Balancing Rational Mind and Emotional Mind to create Wise Mind. Clients can be more mindful and effective when they use both Rational and Emotional Mind. Be sure that clients aren't judging Rational Mind as good and Emotional Mind as bad. By being in *Wise Mind*, clients are in balance and have all their senses, ways of knowing and skills at their disposal to manage their lives effectively and to act in their own best interest.

Distress Tolerance Skills

ACCEPTS	Have clients distract themselves with:
	    Activities
	    Choices
	    Contributions
	    Emotions
	    Pushing away
	    Thoughts
	    Sensations

Crisis Survival Network	It is important for everyone to have a *Crisis Survival Network*. Hopefully, your clients each have one and you are not the only one on it. Educate your clients about who is helpful to have on their list and people who make things worse. Having as many people as possible on the list, and using them flexibly, are key to making this skill most useful.
Half Smile	Have the client find something in their day or in their life that can give them a genuine *Half Smile*. It can be: • A good cup of coffee • Blue sky • Payday • A long weekend coming up • A pleasant memory • The joy on a child's face When a client has a half smile, they are a bit more relaxed in their face, neck and shoulders. Additionally, people respond differently to someone with a smile than to someone who is angry or upset. If the client is treated nicely because they are smiling, that might improve their day a little bit more.

IMPROVE	This acronym provides a series of things for the client to focus on that will distract them from a crisis or stressful situation. Clients can take their time with this one, which will give their nervous systems time to settle down.
	    Imagery of a beautiful or safe place
	  Find **M**eaning in my life
	    Prayer
	    Relaxation
	    One thing at a time
	    Vacation from the demands of my life
	    Encouragement to be effective

Distress Tolerance Skills

Keeping It In Perspective	Ask the client if this is the worst crisis they have ever had to deal with. Typically, they will answer this affirmatively. If so, you can use the metaphor of a marathon: all their other crises and difficulties have been training for this one. The client is now in the best shape of their life, and they are well experienced and can deal with this crisis effectively.
Radical Acceptance	Clients will reduce stress and increase functioning by learning they can control themselves in terms of their thoughts, feelings and actions.
	Although they don't have control over what happens around them or what others do, they can effectively focus their attention and energy on what they can control and change: themselves. This is similar to the Serenity Prayer, which emphasizes having wisdom to know the difference between what you can and can't control.
Self-Soothe Kit	This one can be quite creative. The client puts together a kit that is self-soothing. This can be a physical box they decorate, fill with items that soothe them and keep in a desk at work, in the glove compartment of a car, in a nightstand at home or wherever they find it most useful for them. Ideally, clients include something to soothe all five of their senses.
	This can also be an electronic kit with soothing pictures, music, apps, etc., that they store on their phone or computer.
	Things in the *Self-Soothe Kit* must be effective and not harmful in any way.

Distress Tolerance Skills

SPECIFIC PATHS	This acronym helps clients stay on the path to build the life they want for themselves. What is my **S**upreme concern? **P**ractice my skills Focus my **E**nergy and **C**oncentration **I** can be effective Have **F**aith Consider what is **I**mportant Have **C**ourage and **P**atience Pay **A**ttention Complete **T**asks Be **H**umble Have **S**ensitivity
Turning the Mind	This skill teaches clients that they are in the driver's seat of their mind, including their thoughts, feelings, impulses and even behavior. Clients can first identify which road they are driving on. Then they can choose to stay on the same road; to turn in a different direction by changing their thoughts, feelings, impulses or behavior; to start over by making a "U-turn" or to stop driving for a while and take a break.
Willingness	*Willingness* is open and accepting. It is life-enhancing, energy-generating and relationship-enhancing. By comparison, willfulness is acting like a 2-year-old: wanting what we want even when it isn't in our best interest or does us harm. Willfulness is exhausting, harms relationships and reduces quality of life. *Willingness* exercises are helpful in the middle of a crisis. Clients can practice *Willingness* to accept reality, a bad day, things not going their way or the fact they can't control others and the world around them.

Emotion Regulation Skills

ABC	Using this acronym helps clients to achieve balance in the face of difficult situations. When the client is having a bad day or something unpleasant occurs, they can use this skill to remind themselves of positive things they are good at and use strategies they have prepared for just such occasions. **A**ccumulate positives **B**uild mastery **C**ope ahead
BEHAVIOR	This acronym is useful for clients who want to focus on healing versus hurting behavior or those who are strongly connected to a value system. If the client doesn't like the meaning of a particular letter, they can change it to something else as long as it is effective in being prosocial and well-adjusted. Use effective **B**ehavior Be grounded in the **E**nvironment Do things that are **H**ealing not hurting **A**ct in my best interest Be consistent with my **V**alues **I**magine getting through difficulties Focus on the desired **O**utcome **R**einforce my successes
CARES	This acronym is short, making it easy to remember. This skill is useful for clients who need to modulate their arousal response. Manage my emotions by being **C**alm Monitoring **A**rousal Finding **R**elaxation and rest Coping with my **E**motions and Getting a healthy amount of **S**leep
EMOTIONS	This acronym is concrete and straightforward, which is useful for some clients. **E**xposure to emotions **M**indful of current emotions **O**utline a plan to deal with emotions **T**ake opposite action **I**ncrease positive experiences Identify **O**bstacles and plan to overcome them **N**otice what is going on Use my **S**upport system

Emotion Regulation Skills

Feeling Not Acting	Feeling a strong impulse or emotion is not the same as acting on it. Clients can use their *Moment to Pause* skill to identify and feel an impulse or urge; then they can choose to engage in the impulse, use a skill to manage it or tolerate it while doing nothing.
Lemonade	This skill has clients refocus their weaknesses, problematic thinking and behavior into strengths. When a client has skills and strengths, but may be using them in a way that causes harm or problems in their life, they can take these skills and strengths and focus them differently in their life. For example, an identity thief who becomes a security expert; a car thief who works with police and insurance companies to reduce auto theft; the substance user who gets into recovery and becomes an addictions counselor. A smaller adjustment might be taking the persistence a client demonstrates when declining participation in group therapy and applying it to job searching. With this skill, clients learn they don't have to start over. They learn that while some changes may be required, they don't have to be overwhelmed with trying to be completely different.
Love Dandelions	This skill provides clients with the opportunity to accept themselves or to love their "shadow selves." Clients build awareness and acceptance of the parts of themselves they dislike or find unattractive. Although there are some things they can't change about themselves, by being aware of them, they can minimize damage and distress.
MEDDSS	This skill is all about daily self-care. Self-care dramatically enhances one's emotional well-being. **M**astery **E**xercise **D**iet **D**rugs (Take prescription drugs as directed, but not illicit ones) **S**leep **S**pirituality

Emotion Regulation Skills

Opposite to Emotion	First, ask the client what strong emotion they have that is problematic or troublesome. Ask the client to be mindfully present with this emotion, but not to act on it. Next, ask the client to identify the opposite emotion to the strong emotion. Then ask the client when they naturally feel the opposite emotion. Finally, have the client identify four to six things that they can do on any given day to bring the opposite emotion into their awareness. After this has been established, give the client the assignment that whenever they are feeling a strong, problematic emotion, to hold it in their awareness and actively engage in activities to bring the opposite emotion into their awareness as well.
Ride the Wave	This skill uses the metaphor that the tide comes and goes, but it is always with us just like our emotions and strong impulses. Some days are stormy and chaotic while other days are calmer. While it might feel like a certain emotional state may last forever, it will eventually shift and change into the next emotion. A visualization or artwork exercise could be useful. Direct the client to imagine they are riding the wave of their emotions, using the image of surfing, snowboarding, skiing or skateboarding. Some clients enjoy the feeling of chaos or drama these activities evoke because it is what they know. Similar to the metaphor of surfing, snowboarding, skiing or skateboarding, it is a lot more fun to engage in these activities when the situation is intense than when it's calm. And to do it well, the client has to be fully in the moment. This creates a sense of challenge to manage the intensity of the client's experience, rather than a sense of dread. This skill seems to resonate with teenagers and young adults.

Interpersonal Effectiveness Skills

4 Horsemen of the Apocalypse	Criticism, contempt, defensiveness and stonewalling may be the four most destructive behaviors in relationships. If a client has these four "horsemen" in their relationship, then the relationship might be over. The above behaviors may not apply to all clients. Each client can identify their own "horsemen" and then implement strategies to keep these destructive forces out of their relationships. Other horsemen might be:
Broken Record	The client practices being a broken record with themselves: they keep coming back to their needs and wants.
Dealing with Difficult People	This skill teaches clients to be nonjudgmental, participate in improving their relationships and identify and overcome obstacles to improvement. Suggested steps include: • Describe my relationship nonjudgmentally • Be empowered to make changes myself and accept that I can't change the other person • Explore my particular sensitivity to this relationship

DEAR SELF	This skill is used to accomplish a task or meet an objective.
	
	      Describe what I want
	   Be **E**ncouraging
	      Ask for what is wanted
	      Reinforce others
	      Sometimes tolerating not getting my way
	      Experiencing the present moment mindfully, inside and outside my body
	      Listening skillfully to myself and others
	      Finding negotiation opportunities

FAST	Self-respect is the goal of this skill. This skill helps clients who are out of balance with codependency or who focus on others to also focus on themselves.
	
	   Be **F**air to myself
	      Apologize less
	      Stick to my values
	   Be **T**ruthful with myself

The table embedded in the "4 Horsemen of the Apocalypse" section:

Youth	Adults
Not communicating	Dishonesty
Withdrawal	Out-of-control spending
Dishonesty	Credit card debt
School refusal	Working too much
Playing video games	Drugs and alcohol
Bullying and violence	Violence
Drugs and alcohol	Infidelity
Delinquency	Internet sex/pornography

Interpersonal Effectiveness Skills

GIVE	This skill is designed to provide clients with methods to improve and sustain relationships in healthy ways. Be **G**entle in relationships **I**nterested **V**alidating and Have an **E**asy manner with others
Relationship Assumptions	This skill puts the dialectical philosophy into the language of couples or families. 1. Both of us are doing the best we can. 2. Both of us can be more effective. 3. Both of us want to be more effective. 4. Both of us have to be more effective, try harder and apply our skills. 5. Neither of us caused all the problems in our relationship, and we both must work together to solve them.
Relationship Mindfulness	Clients can apply mindfulness to their relationships using this skill. • Identify generalizations • Describe assumptions • Suspend judgments • Avoid jumping to conclusions • Be empowered in relationships • Participate and communicate effectively
Repairs	Many clients probably grew up, or are currently growing up, in families who didn't teach them how to make healthy *Repairs*. Making *Repairs* is about taking responsibility, apologizing when appropriate, accepting an apology when it makes sense, having the ability to let go and move on and learning from the situation to avoid it in the future.
Turn the Tables	Gifts given without strings attached are the most satisfying gifts to give. When clients give expecting something in return—even without consciously stating they expect reciprocity—they often end up very dissatisfied. This skill helps clients let go of this expectation and do things for other people without needing anything in return.

Chapter 4

Teaching the Skills

Many of the suggestions in this section will apply not only to teaching DBT skills, but also to teaching other psychoeducational models or skills. Learning needs to be accessible, relevant, engaging, fun and interesting. Two major considerations for teaching skills are learning styles and attention spans. When providing psychoeducation programs like DBT, it is essential that the clinician attend to these considerations.

LEARNING STYLES

Children, teenagers and adults learn three ways—auditorily, visually and kinesthetically—and each person has a preferred style or way they learn best. If clients learn best by listening and talking about things, they are primarily auditory learners. On the other hand, if clients learn best through reading and visual representations, they are primarily visual learners. Finally, there are clients who learn best by doing things, being active and practicing things in their lives. These clients are kinesthetic learners. While each person has a preferred style or way they learn best, most clients can benefit from learning new concepts through a variety of styles.

When teaching DBT skills, it is important to appeal to all three of these styles. Lecture or discussions about the skills are helpful, as is providing visual representations of skills through media, posters or objects.

Examples of auditory learning activities	Examples of visual learning activities	Examples of kinesthetic learning activities
• Lecture • Discussion • Small group exercises	• Written handouts • PowerPoint presentations • Art projects • Games	• Art projects • Games • Role-plays • Small group exercises

Perhaps the most important component of learning DBT is practice. There is a difference between knowing a skill and using a skill. Some clients can learn skills quickly; they may be able to provide a sophisticated explanation of them, and even coach or give advice to their peers. However, all of this can happen without the client practicing the skill in their life on a consistent basis. Therefore, it's important that clients practice the skills in the session, whether it is individual or group format, as well as in their daily lives.

An example of this occurred when a client enrolled in a treatment program with a significant DBT focus. This client enrolled in treatment because she was having problems with addiction, out-of-control relationships, and impaired parenting. The client had previously participated in a DBT group at another treatment center and she brought her old treatment binder to the first session of her new group. Throughout the whole first session, she did not participate. At the end of the group, she approached the group clinician and said she didn't think she should have to participate since she had been through DBT before. She even pulled out her binder to prove she had gone through DBT. Her reasoning was that participating in the group was similar to taking a college course: she had taken the group at another center, so she should receive credit for the work she already completed.

The group clinician listened to her reasoning and looked at the work she had completed; then proceeded to ask questions about how she was using one or two of the skills, and also asked for examples of how the skills had been helpful with her recent troubles. The client was able to name the skills and sometimes gave accurate definitions of them, but she was unable to give a coherent example or demonstrate how she was using the skills. The clinician commented that she certainly had done some work in a previous group, thanked the client for sharing her treatment work and then suggested she could benefit from more practice and integration of the skills into her life.

The client was somewhat unhappy with this response. She then pleaded her case to her individual clinician. This clinician was aware of her request to the group clinician and took more time to process the request with the client. The client was again unable to give examples in sufficient detail to demonstrate the use of DBT skills in her daily life. The clinician validated the client's request and then explained that the continued difficulties in her life and her present unhappiness could probably be alleviated by her increased use of many of the skills. In doing so, the clinician maintained a balance by using the therapeutic dialectics of:

- Acceptance and Change
- Centeredness and Flexibility
- Nurturing and Benevolently Demanding

The clinician suggested that the client was using the skill of *Broken Record* by making multiple requests to get a need met. Then the clinician encouraged the client to use the *Lemonade* skill instead, by refocusing her persistence and using her ability to ask for accommodations in ways that would serve her better and bring her more success. Through the therapeutic relationship and irreverent and supportive communication, the client could enter a contract to stay in the group and to focus on using the skills in her life.

Later in treatment, the client commented that she had thought she knew the skills and was using them, but she'd realized she wasn't using them as much as she could. Upon coming to this realization, she could discuss in considerable detail different DBT skills and act out several of the skills she had found particularly helpful. Furthermore, she became an ally of the group clinician by encouraging other clients and pointing out discrepancies that demonstrated when clients might not be using the skills as much as they could be.

Attention Span

Although some clients may have very long attention spans, everyone's attention span is limited in nature. Some activities can engage clients' attention spans for extended amounts of time, while other activities are only able to engage their attention spans for a few minutes or seconds. When teaching the skills, it is optimal to have a variety of activities and not to do any one activity for too long. If the clinician is bored with an activity, the clients may be bored as well. A general rule of thumb is 15–20 minutes of focused work or instruction before taking a five-minute micro-break or switching to an engaging activity. Activities to try include:

- Video and music examples
- Handouts
- Small-group activities

- Skits and charades
- Artwork such as painting, modeling clay or making collages
- Having the clients teach one another a skill (in group sessions)
- Imagery and visualizations
- Role-plays and in vivo practice
- Guest speakers

Observe and learn from the clients, and use what works for them. Learn from professional colleagues as well: inquire how other clinicians teach skills, watch other clinicians work or invite other clinicians to the group. DBT is hard work and having fun is a useful way to make it engaging and interesting.

Additional components to consider when teaching DBT skills include fostering motivation, tools that foster learning and cognitive-behavioral interventions. Practice and homework assignments outside the individual or group therapy session are also essential if clients are going to be successful in utilizing their DBT skills in real-life situations.

MOTIVATIONAL STRATEGIES

Part of the DBT focus is on maintaining a dialectical balance between self-interest and investing in relationships with others. Self-interest in moderation can be very effective. An essential piece of building client motivation to engage in DBT is finding out what is important to the client: their values, goals and who they want to be. The following list provides some examples of things that are important to clients, and these are often framed in the negative:

Positive Frame	Negative Frame
Being pain-free	Having too much pain
Emotional stability	Emotionally out of control
Clarity of thought	Confusion
Self-knowledge	Feeling out of touch with oneself
Being respected	Being disrespected
Being loved	Being disliked, hated or alone
Loving others	Disliking or hating others
Functional family	"Crazy" family
Strong support system	Problematic or no support system
Financial independence	Debt or dependence on others
Stable, appropriate employment	Under- or unemployment
Stimulating career	Directionless or passionless career
Creative outlets	Feeling unimaginative or uninspired
Recreation and leisure	Bored with nothing to do
Ethics and morality	No guiding principles
Contributing to others' lives, local environment or global community	Isolation

Values are an important component to building motivation. A client may want to be a "good" person, parent, family member, student, employee, etc. Values might include doing the right thing, being the best person they can be, contributing through service work, volunteerism and charity, as well as a connection with spiritual practices. By taking the client's values into consideration and weaving them into the clinical process, a clinician can help clients to build insight into how DBT's life perspective fits for them, and determine which skills will work in their lives. Skills to support values include *Nonjudgmental, Wise Mind, Keeping It In Perspective* and *BEHAVIOR*.

Most clients also have a variety of goals they want to accomplish. When the clinician shows clients how they can use their skills to achieve their goals, they will see what is in it for them. Using the skill *Effectively* encourages clients to be efficient and intentional with their efforts. *Effectively* also helps a client keep their eye on the proverbial ball by avoiding distraction or undermining their own efforts. Other skills that are useful for accomplishing goals are *Lemonade, Turning the Mind* and *FAST*.

Get to know what clients consider important and tailor the DBT skills and philosophy to assist them in achieving these goals. If they need to increase one or more things they consider important, choose skills that will help them to accomplish this. If the client believes they have already met several of these goals or values, focus on developing the skills to maintain those values.

For instance, if a client wants to have more emotional stability, most of the Emotion Regulation skills are helpful—particularly *Ride the Wave*. If the client has established emotional stability and wants to maintain it, the clinician might suggest using *MEDDSS* daily and *Keeping It In Perspective* when indicated. In the case of a client who wants to establish clarity of thought, the clinician might suggest *Wise Mind*; and when a client wants to maintain clarity of thought, focus on *Turning the Mind* and *Broken Record*.

Furthermore, the clinician can help the client to build a strong support system by teaching the skill of *Relationship Mindfulness*, or help the client sustain healthy relationships by utilizing the skills of *Repairs* and *4 Horsemen of the Apocalypse*. Creative outlets, fun and recreational opportunities can be increased by using the skill *ABC*; and maintaining creative outlets, fun and recreational opportunities can be accomplished by using *Half Smile* and *IMPROVES*. Finally, the skills of *Willingness* and *Radical Acceptance* would be useful to increase values, and using *BEHAVIOR* and *Turtling* are beneficial to maintain skills in the areas of ethics and morality. These are just a few suggestions of skills. However, the clinician might choose different skills based on the situation, the unique aspects of the client and the clinician's own judgment.

Although it may be challenging to get clients to envision the future when they are in pain, engaging in unhealthy relationships or problematic or life-threatening behavior, empowering clients to be who they want to be taps into their hope, optimism and vision for the future. One strategy is to start small. Help the client to achieve a small success and then build on it by using two Motivational Interviewing (MI) techniques: hypothetical change and radical change (Miller & Rollnick, 2012).

Hypothetical Change

Hypothetical change is a useful intervention for clients who can't imagine how their lives could be any different. This intervention entails asking the client how someone in a similar situation in another time or another place could change their life to be completely different. This might sound something like: "Hypothetically, let's say there is someone who looks a little like you and has a life similar to yours in a parallel universe. How would you assist this person to make the necessary changes in thinking, feeling and behaving to reach their potential and be the person they want to be?"

This approach engages clients in finding their own solutions and helps get them out of typical hopeless perspectives. It also gives them the opportunity to think outside the box, suspend barriers and obstacles and focus only on solutions. Moreover, they will also experience a sense of pride in being able to provide advice and assistance to others, even if only hypothetically.

Radical Change

The second strategy is radical change. Radical change is about envisioning that everything is different and any or all change is possible. A common therapeutic technique that illustrates radical change is the miracle question, which sounds something like: "If you woke up tomorrow and all your problems were solved, what would your life look like?" or "Let's say that on your birthday (or January 1), you will be the person you want to be. Who would that person be?"

When using either hypothetical or radical change, once the client has a vision of who they want to be or what they want their life to look like, the clinician and client work together to develop a plan to accomplish their vision. The plan needs to be both detailed and flexible. Help the client set the stage for success by setting small steps they can accomplish and normalizing difficulties. One skill that is useful here is *Keeping It In Perspective.* Similarly, the *Lemonade* skill lets a client tap into their unused potential and channel it in an effective manner to implement their vision. For example, a client who tolerates considerable emotional or physical pain when self-harming can channel this ability to tolerate pain by using it to work hard and endure disappointments and setbacks.

Rolling with Resistance

In addition to hypothetical and radical change, there are several other MI techniques that are useful in building motivation for change and for integrating DBT philosophy and skills into daily life (Miller & Rollnick, 2012). One underlying principle of MI that is particularly important is the process of rolling with resistance, in which the clinician takes a nonjudgmental stance when responding to any resistance that clients bring into the therapeutic process. Rolling with resistance includes eight interventions that can be divided in two categories: supportive and strategic.

Supportive rolling with resistance interventions include simple, amplified and double-sided reflections. Reflection involves repeating to a client what they have just communicated or have communicated in the past, whether verbally or nonverbally. Reflections can repeat the client's communication identically or nearly so. In a *Simplified Reflection,* clinicians rephrase or paraphrase client communication by using different words with very similar meanings. An *Amplified Reflection* intensifies the client's statement or focuses on a particular piece; while a *Double-Sided Reflection* acknowledges what the client has said, as well as other sides of the situation. Reflecting back the client's emotions or feelings is another way to use this type of interaction.

Simplified Reflections let the client know that the clinician understands them by reflecting back what the clinician hears or sees.

> **Client:** "I don't see how this will help me."

> **Clinician:** "You can't imagine how this will make your life better."

Amplified Reflections are when a clinician adds emphasis or weight to a piece of the client's communication.

> **Client:** "I've tried stuff like this before and it never seems to work for long. I get exhausted having to work so hard. I wish my life were different and I didn't have so many problems. It doesn't seem fair that others don't have it as hard as I do."

Clinician: "You've worked really hard. You've put a lot of effort into changing your life, but it still remains the same."

Double-Sided Reflections explicitly acknowledge dialectics by bringing in both, or many, sides of how the client feels or thinks about something.

Client: "I really wish it wasn't so hard. I want my life to be better, but I don't want to have to do all this work. Shouldn't I be better by now? When I started I was so hopeful you could solve this for me and my life would be perfect."

Clinician: "So there is part of you that wants things to be better and another part of you that doesn't want to work so hard. You wish there was a way to change things and you had hoped I could make everything all right."

Reflections demonstrate to the client that the clinician is paying attention and understands. They also foster the therapeutic relationship and validate the client. Once there is trust and a strong working relationship, the clinician can utilize strategic rolling with resistance techniques. These techniques include *Reframing*, *Agreement with a Twist*, *Shifting Focus*, *Emphasizing Personal Choice and Control* and *Coming Alongside* (*Paradox*).

Reframing changes the meaning of what the client is talking about to help them see that change would be helpful.

Client: "I've tried a lot of things. I already know how to make things better."

Clinician: "So you have a lot of information and skills, we just need to figure out how to use them most effectively."

Agreement with a Twist is a reflection with a reframe. First, the clinician reflects what the client is communicating and then reframes it.

Client: "There's no point. My life will never be better."

Clinician: "It feels like everything is hopeless and that things will never improve. I remember you telling me in the past you didn't think your life would get better, but then you really started to make changes. In the past, you have taken hopelessness and turned it into energy and commitment to finding a way to live life differently."

Shifting Focus is a useful intervention when the client feels overwhelmed, hopeless or defensive. This entails changing the subject to a less intense or provocative subject—at least for a little while.

Client: "Why do we keep talking about this? This isn't helping me. What are you doing to help me? This feels like a complete waste of my time."

Clinician: "Maybe now isn't the time to talk about doing this differently. I remember at the beginning of the session you wanted to tell me about what a great weekend you had. Tell me more about that."

Emphasizing Personal Choice and Control puts the client in the driver's seat, much like the skill of *Turning the Mind*. Clients learn it is up to them and that they have the ability to do it their way. This intervention is particularly useful for clients who feel forced into treatment, or in cases where there is an explicit mandate.

Client: "I don't see why I have to be here. There's nothing you can tell me that will make a difference."

Clinician: "Being here seems pointless. It's really up to you to figure out how being here will be useful, what you want to learn, and how you might do things differently in your life."

Coming Alongside is a paradoxical intervention. Here the clinician predicts the client cannot do it differently. This intervention is sometimes judged as manipulative, and it doesn't work for some clinicians and certain clients. Passive, dependent clients probably won't get the most out of this technique, but clients who are anti-authority, who need to be right and who are contrary by nature often respond well to this intervention.

Client: "There's no point, I can't get it right. I'll never be successful."

Clinician: "Staying the same seems to be the only option. You couldn't do it even if you really tried hard."

For more information on MI see: *Motivational Interviewing* by William R. Miller and Stephen Rollnick (2012).

Transtheoretical Model

A model related to MI that is useful for increasing client's effective behavior is the Transtheoretical Model (Prochaska & DiClemente, 1983; Prochaska, DiClemente, & Norcross 1992), also mentioned in Chapter 2. The Transtheoretical Model is used to identify a client's readiness for change by evaluating which of the SOC a client is in and using appropriate interventions for that specific SOC to facilitate forward movement (Prochaska & Prochaska, 2016). The Stages of Change include *pre-contemplation, contemplation, preparation, action, maintenance* and *relapse*. Since change is a dynamic process, it is most useful to consider the junctures between stages as the client moves from one stage to another. The junctures are:

- *Early Pre-Contemplation*

- *Late Pre-Contemplation → Early Contemplation*

- *Late Contemplation → Early Preparation*

- *Late Preparation → Early Action*

- *Late Action → Early Maintenance*

- *Early Maintenance → Late Maintenance*

- *Relapse* or *return to old behavior*

In *Early Pre-Contemplation,* clients do not think they have a problem. Interventions to facilitate forward movement in this stage are those that support clients' strengths, explore goals and raise awareness of problems and difficulties.

Suggested DBT skills: *Willingness* and *Pros & Cons*

In *Late Pre-Contemplation → Early Contemplation,* clients have an emerging awareness of their problem and begin to think about how to deal with it. Interventions to facilitate forward movement include normalizing that change is overwhelming at times, leveraging environmental and relational reasons for change and tapping into previous successes.

Suggested DBT skill: *Turtling*

In *Late Contemplation → Early Preparation,* clients think about change and begin to create a plan to make change happen. Interventions to facilitate forward movement include fostering intrapsychic reasons for change, tapping into clients' self-efficacy and lowering obstacles to making a change.

Suggested DBT skill: *Lemonade*

In *Late Preparation → Early Action,* clients continue to make plans to change and they begin to engage in behaviors to put change into place. Interventions to facilitate forward movement include announcing change plans, enlisting interpersonal support, and establishing success through small changes that come easily to the client.

Suggested DBT skill: *Observe, Describe & Participate*

In *Late Action → Early Maintenance,* clients engage in continued efforts to change and begin to maintain changes that have been accomplished. Forward movement is facilitated by positively reinforcing the changes made, planning for challenging situations that provoke a return to old behaviors and supporting the client's resolve to have a different life.

Suggested DBT skill: *SPECIFIC PATHS*

In *Early Maintenance → Late Maintenance,* clients maintain the changes that they have made and are adopting these changes into their daily life. Interventions to use here include those that illustrate self-efficacy, support effective problem-solving abilities and normalize bumps in the road.

Suggested DBT skill: *Effectively*

Relapse or return to old behavior involves returning to problematic or self-injurious behavior, or returning to old systems. Sometimes clients actively engage in their relapse, and sometimes relapse happens to them—particularly regarding mental health symptoms. Relapse can happen at any time during the change process. When a client is on the road to relapse or has relapsed, the clinician can leverage the therapeutic relationship, evaluate factors leading to the relapse, and support the client's self-efficacy to reinstitute their DBT skills.

Suggested DBT skill: *Turtling*

For more information on Stages of Change, see: *Changing for Good: A Revolutionary Six-Stage Program for Overcoming Bad Habits and Moving Your Life Positively Forward* by James O. Prochaska, John Norcross and Carlo DiClemente (1994).

Motivational strategies address the fundamental question of why a client should be interested in learning DBT skills. Motivation to learn about DBT skills should never be assumed. If a client doesn't view learning certain information or skills as relevant to their needs or desires, then the client will not be motivated to invest the necessary effort into learning and practicing the skills.

Developing client motivation to learn information and skills is critical for teaching each DBT module. Motivational strategies involve helping clients see how learning information and skills will help them achieve short- and long-term goals, such as the reduction of distress due to mental health symptoms, hopelessness and destructive behaviors, or improving relationships, employment or volunteer opportunities, recreational activities or other desired changes.

Developing this motivation is an ongoing and collaborative process that occurs throughout treatment. Motivation can wax and wane over time, especially if clients perceive their goals to be distant and difficult to achieve. For that reason, motivation often needs to be rechecked or rekindled in the midst of teaching information or skills—even if motivation may have been previously established. To help clients sustain motivation, clinicians need to convey their own confidence that clients can achieve their goals and support clients' optimism, self-confidence and self-efficacy.

COGNITIVE-BEHAVIORAL STRATEGIES

Cognitive-behavioral strategies involve the systematic application of learning principles to help clients acquire and use DBT information and skills. A number of different cognitive-behavioral strategies are employed in helping clients master DBT skills.

Reinforcement

Reinforcement can be broken down into two types: positive reinforcement and negative reinforcement. In positive reinforcement, a motivating item is presented that increases the likelihood of a behavior being repeated. Examples of positive reinforcers include receiving a gift or reward, praise by a partner or close friend, or more time spent in a situation. In negative reinforcement, behavior or consequences are removed in order to increase the likelihood of a specific outcome. Examples of negative reinforcers include anxiety, being hungover, "nagging" by a partner or being "grounded" from technology. Negative reinforcement should not be confused with punishment, which is something unpleasant and intentionally imposed by an external authority in response to behavior.

The principles of reinforcement play an important role in DBT because its core goals are, by their very nature, reinforcing. For example, DBT skills are positively reinforcing when the client experiences success, empowerment, improvement in relationships and increased life satisfaction. Similarly, DBT skills are negatively reinforcing when the client undergoes fewer difficulties and experiences decreased distress and pain. Moreover, the clinician provides positive reinforcement in the form of cheerleading and encouragement, which acknowledges clients' efforts and makes them feel a sense of self-efficacy.

As a client learns and applies the skills taught in DBT, they accomplish more of their goals and live consistently with their values. As they begin to experience the life they want to live and become the person they want to be, skill use is reinforced, both positively and negatively, which encourages continued use of the skills. Clinicians need to work closely with clients and monitor progress toward goals to ensure these positive outcomes of DBT are maintained.

Shaping

Shaping refers to the reinforcement of successive approximations to a goal. The expression "Rome wasn't built in a day" summarizes the concept of shaping. Like the building of Rome, the information and skills taught in DBT take time to learn, with each client learning at their own pace. Practicing complex skills—such as *Nonjudgmental*, *Radical Acceptance* and *Opposite to Emotion*—and using the acronyms can truly help clients to understand and integrate these skills into their lives. It is important for the clinician to recognize the steps taken along the way and to provide ample positive feedback and encouragement. Even when the pace of learning is quite slow and each step forward is small, clinicians can acknowledge these gains by pointing them out, praising efforts, and letting clients know they are making progress. Taking a "shaping attitude" means clinicians understand the amount of time and effort required to learn the information and DBT skills, and provide frequent reinforcement to clients as they progress.

Modeling

One of the most powerful methods for teaching someone a skill is to demonstrate it. Modeling has an important role to play in teaching DBT, especially in helping clients learn new skills. When modeling a new skill, it is useful for the clinician to first describe the nature of the skill and then to explain that it will be demonstrated to show how it works. The clinician then models the skill and, when completed, obtains feedback from the client about what they observed and how effective the skill appeared to be.

To model skill use, the clinician can also tell a story about how they used a skill in their own life (without disclosing too much personal information), or about someone they knew who used a skill. They can also ask if the client knows anyone who appears to have used the skill being taught. In addition, the clinician can act out or demonstrate situations where their client would use these skills in real life. Modeling the skill in a variety of ways can give clients concrete examples of how to use the skill and allow them to see the benefits of using it.

Behavioral Tailoring

Behavioral tailoring involves helping clients develop strategies to incorporate skills and behaviors that will serve them well in their daily lives. As clients learn the DBT skills, they can work with the clinician to determine the skills that are most useful to them, and develop a plan to integrate these skills into their day-to-day experiences. Building the application of skills and desired behaviors into an existing routine will provide clients with regular cues to use their skills, thereby minimizing the chances that they will forget to do so.

Interest in using skills, or in applying the desired behavior, can be established by motivational techniques, including eliciting and reviewing the advantages of skill use (e.g., reduced symptoms, and fewer relapses and/or re-hospitalizations) and making progress toward client goals. Diary cards are also useful with behavioral tailoring.

When using behavioral tailoring, the clinician first explores the client's daily routine, including their self-care regimen, activities of daily living, work, family relationships and recreational pursuits. The clinician and the client then identify an activity that can be adapted to include the application of DBT skills. To ensure that this plan is carried out, the clinician takes the lead and models the routine for the client, and then engages the client in a role-play of the same routine. After rehearsing the routine in session, the clinician and the client establish a homework assignment to implement the plan. Successful implementation of the behavioral tailoring plan is reinforced by praising the client for following through.

Practice and Role-Play

The expression "practice makes perfect" is well-suited to learning DBT skills. Clients need to practice these skills both inside and outside of sessions. This helps clients become more familiar with a DBT skill and identify obstacles to using the skill outside of sessions. It also provides opportunities for feedback from the clinician and others.

Practicing DBT skills in session is especially effective when it is combined with modeling by the clinician. One of the best methods to help clients practice a DBT skill is for the clinician to set up a role-play to allow the client to use the skill in the kind of situation that may come up in the client's life. After a skill has been practiced, the clinician should always note some strengths of the client's performance and strive to be as specific as possible. The clinician may also choose to give some suggestions to the client about how the skill may be used even more effectively, and additional practice in the session may be helpful.

It is also important for clients to practice their skills outside of sessions. Clients may be able to learn the skills and even demonstrate the skills in session, but if they don't use them outside of therapy or treatment, they are going to get very little out of them. It is only by practicing skills outside of the sessions that they can improve their abilities to manage their symptoms, reach optimal functioning and increase life satisfaction.

Homework Assignments

Giving clients homework assignments between sessions is essential to helping them practice their DBT skills on their own, outside of session. After all, there is a difference between knowing skills and using them. When clients practice the skills—even when they don't have an urgent need to use the skills—they are more likely to be able to use those skills in a high-stress situation. For these reasons, clinicians must assign practice homework.

One homework assignment that requires the client to demonstrate the use of DBT skills is keeping diary cards. Diary cards ask the client to track their use of skills by having them record the number of times they use a skill. This can be a tally in the client's daily planner, check marks in their checkbook register, on their smartphone—whatever works for the client. It is human nature to do more of something when we are counting it and want to increase it.

The reverse also works when trying to decrease or reduce something. An example of reducing something is the "swear jar." If children are using profanity or swear words, their parents can start a swear jar that requires the children to pay each time they swear. Their increased awareness, and the actual cost of swearing, will help children to reduce their swearing significantly. The same principle applies to using DBT skills. The more the client tracks the use of their skills, as well as the behaviors to be reduced or eliminated, the more often the skills will be used, and the less often the unhelpful or harmful behaviors will occur.

Diary cards are also useful to the clinician because they show what skills the client is using and how often. When clients use the skills and document this on their diary cards, the clinician can positively reinforce the skill use and hear success stories. If there are difficulties using the skills, the clinician can also work with the client to reduce or eliminate the difficulties.

It is common for clients to forget to complete their diary cards at first. However, it is important to continue to hold the expectation of completing the cards. If the clinician lets a client "off the hook" for keeping up with the cards, then that client will get less out of DBT and run the risk of not implementing the skills in their life at all.

In addition, not practicing the skills between sessions and failing to complete diary cards are considered major therapy-interfering behaviors (see Chapter 2). If the clinician fails to hold the client responsible and invests in the client's agenda, the clinician reinforces the notion that skills and diary cards aren't important. It is essential to avoid this message. Clinicians need to acknowledge these therapy-interfering behaviors, address the issues, hold the client accountable and reinforce maintaining the diary cards by limiting the focus on the client's agenda until there is adequate investment in practicing skills and completing the cards.

Relapse Prevention

Relapse can be defined as a return of symptoms or difficulties, re-engaging in self-destructive behavior, or using alcohol or other drugs. Sometimes clients actively participate in their relapses by not taking medications, reducing self-care efforts, re-engaging in problematic relationships or in self-harming behavior, or using substances. At other times, relapses occur for reasons out of the client's control, such as the cyclical nature of bipolar and seasonal affective disorders. Relapses can also be brought on by environmental stressors, such as losing a job or income source, family member illness, cars breaking down or losing housing.

Relapse prevention is about helping the client identify warning signs of returning to old, problematic behaviors, and developing a plan to avoid or minimize a relapse. For instance, the client can enlist a support system to assist them in watching for warning signs. When a warning sign has been identified, the client can utilize a variety of DBT skills, receive support from family and friends, attend community support meetings, or talk with their clinician. Even if the client relapses to their old behavior or begins to use substances, it is still better to catch it as soon as possible so the client can intervene quickly and effectively before the relapse is full-blown or drawn out.

Developing effective relapse prevention plans requires knowledge of, and success with, DBT skills. When developing these plans, the clinician guides clients through a discussion of what a relapse might look like, what could bring it on, and how to avoid a relapse. As part of this process, it is useful to review any previous relapses the client may have experienced and highlight any client insights or clinician observations to minimize future relapses. An informal relapse prevention plan template is as follows:

Warning Sign: _____

DBT Skill: _____

Outcome: _____

(If warning sign continues or worsens, contact support system or a helping professional.)

Recovery Planning

A strengths-based parallel to relapse-prevention planning is recovery planning. Since DBT is designed to empower clients to build a life worth living, it makes sense that most clinicians would develop a recovery plan with their clients. An example of a suggested plan follows.

Recovery Plan

Recovery is about being the best possible person and reaching your potential while effectively dealing with stress and difficulties—such as mental health and substance use problems. It involves effectively relying on family and support systems, maintaining life roles, engaging in meaningful activities, finding time for recreational opportunities and having fun—to name just a few.

This is my plan for recovery and optimal functioning:

Which DBT skills are most helpful for me?

_____

_____

1. **Practicing MEDDSS daily establishes a healthy self-care regimen.**

   Mastery Activities: What are activities I do well and that make me feel positive?

   _____

   _____

   Exercise: What type of exercise can I engage in?

   _____

   _____

   Diet: Which healthy foods could I increase in my diet?

   _____

   _____

   Drugs: What are my current medications and dosages?

   _____

   _____

   Sleeping: How much sleep do I need to function at my best?

   _____

   _____

   Spirituality: In what ways can I engage in my spiritual practice(s) daily?

   _____

   _____

2. **Prevention of relapse or return to old problematic behavior.**

   The most important warning signs of problems reoccurring are:

   _____

   _____

When I first notice the warning signs, I will use the following DBT skills:

_____

_____

3. **Healthy support system.**

These are the people in my support system who support my recovery and use of DBT skills:

_____

_____

4. **Having fun and recreation is an important part of recovery.**

I will ensure that I have time for fun and recreation in my life on a regular basis by using the following strategies:

_____

_____

These are the fun and recreational activities I will participate in on a regular basis to support my recovery:

_____

_____

I will utilize community support meetings by:

_____

_____

5. **Dealing with stress.**

The most stressful things in my life are:

_____

_____

I will use the following DBT skills to manage my stress:

_____

_____

6. **Recovery goals.**

What progress have I made toward my recovery?

_____

_____

What am I currently working on in my recovery?

_____

_____

What will I do to maintain positive changes and continue my growth?

_____

_____

Chapter 5

Formats, Settings and Age Groups

DBT can be practiced as an exclusive modality, as a primary model with a few other models, in an integrated manner along with multiple other modalities or on an as-needed basis by using just a few components or skills. For instance, DBT can be integrated in a variety of formats, including individual therapy sessions, group therapy sessions, case management appointments, behavioral health consultations in a PCP office, medication management, outreach visits, recreation activities or by spending unstructured time in the therapeutic community, classroom or at home with family and friends. Each clinician should determine for themselves how much DBT will be integrated into their practice based on their own comfort level and need, and the types of clients they're treating.

Practice setting also has an impact on the amount of DBT used in the clinical process. Private practice clinicians may have the flexibility to choose their therapeutic modalities and interventions, but this may also be influenced by who is paying for treatment: an insurance company, employer, school, family or the client. Private practice clinicians are also accountable to the client—who either explicitly request a specific therapy (such as DBT), or who present with symptoms (such as self-harming behavior), which are known to have positive outcomes with an EBP such as DBT. Clinicians working in a treatment program or facility typically need to provide treatment consistent with regulations, as well as facility philosophy and policies. Fortunately, with its many components, DBT is a model that can be adapted and reorganized to work in a variety of ways.

Individual Sessions

Teaching clients the DBT philosophy and skills can be an integral part of individual sessions. In these sessions, motivation and learning can be tailored specifically to each client. The client's history, and information from previous sessions, can be used as examples of when a client has already used a skill or how a skill could be helpful. Metaphors can also be applied specifically to the client's life.

When using DBT in individual sessions, skills teaching should only be a portion of what is covered. Teaching DBT skills needs to be balanced with the client's agenda, new issues or goals, external mandates and developing the therapeutic relationship. Based on the clinician's training and current practices (as discussed previously), the amount of DBT used in session is also balanced with other perspectives, modalities, interventions and techniques.

There are various ways to integrate DBT skills teaching into individual sessions (see Chapter 4). One method is for the clinician to prepare to teach a specific skill prior to the session. The clinician would then begin the session by checking in with the client and subsequently introducing the skill for that session. After defining the skill, the clinician would ask the client to think about whether they have ever used the skill or whether other people have done so—even if the client didn't know the specific name of the skill or why it was useful. Next, there might be a role-play opportunity or a visualization of how the client could use the skill in their life.

Wrapping up the educational process would include a short exploration of potential barriers to using the skill, along with ways to problem-solve these obstacles. To effectively deal with these barriers and obstacles, it is important for clients to use the DBT skills even when there is no immediate solution to a problem. It is important for clients to know that using any set of skills will be challenging and imperfect;

otherwise they'll be at risk of giving up early when they discover it takes effort and doesn't always work. At the completion of the barriers and obstacles conversation, the clinician can request that the client use the skill as much as possible until the next session, and track their skill use with a diary card.

It is preferable to teach the skill at the beginning of the session for 5 to 20 minutes. Then the rest of the session could be spent on other things the clinician, or client, has on their agenda. When a skill is taught at the beginning of the session, clients typically will reference the skill later in the session when they are talking about what is important to them. As clients reflect on their lives, they might see how the skill could work well for them, or they may remember times they already did something similar to the skill. If the skill is taught at the end of the session, this opportunity is missed, and time might run out before the skill can be fully explored.

Another method to integrate DBT skills into individual sessions is to spontaneously teach a skill based on the issues the client is currently processing. In this instance, the clinician may be listening to the issues the client is presenting and realize that a specific skill would be useful in that situation. At this point, the clinician can dive into teaching the skill if they feel comfortable doing so, or make a note and prepare to teach the skill in the next session. Once the skill has been chosen, the clinician will probably use a process like the previous method.

A third method of incorporating DBT into individual therapy includes developing single or multiple treatment plans with DBT skills as the planned intervention. Here the client's presenting problem is identified, the treatment goal is determined and then an appropriate skill is chosen to meet the goal. The clinician then plans the method of teaching the skill, decides on practice opportunities and selects homework assignments.

Group Therapy

DBT can be taught at least two ways in a group format. The first way involves having a curriculum and a lesson plan for each group. A group curriculum can be dedicated to a specific module—such as a Mindfulness group or an Emotion Regulation group—or it can offer skills from all four modules. Incorporating skills from all modules can be done by either devoting several weeks to the same module:

>Month 1: Mindfulness Skills

>Month 2: Emotion Regulation Skills

>Month 3: Distress Tolerance Skills

>Month 4: Interpersonal Effectiveness Skills

Or by alternating weeks in which a skill is taught from each module:

>Week 1: Mindfulness Skills

>Week 2: Emotion Regulation Skills

>Week 3: Distress Tolerance Skills

>Week 4: Interpersonal Effectiveness Skills

When an entire group or individual session is focused on a DBT skill, the preferred structure is:

First Third of the Session:

- Review homework.

- Have client(s) display how the skill was used.

- Practice skill if the client(s) didn't do the homework.

Second Third of the Session:

- Introduce the new skill.

- Teach the skill with creativity, interaction, and in a way that appeals to all three learning styles.

- Give examples of how to use the skill.

- Ask client(s) if they have had experience with the skill or something similar.

Last Third of the Session:

- Practice or role-play the skill.

- Discuss barriers and obstacles to using the new skill, and how to overcome them effectively.

- Assign the skill as homework to be practiced between now and the next session.

Here is how a four-month curriculum could be organized:

Month 1	Week 1: Mindfulness	*Wise Mind*
	Week 2: Distress Tolerance	*Crisis Survival Network*
	Week 3: Emotion Regulation	*Ride the Wave*
	Week 4: Interpersonal Effectiveness	*Repairs*
Month 2	Week 1: Mindfulness	*Observe, Describe & Participate*
	Week 2: Distress Tolerance	*Self-Soothe Kit*
	Week 3: Emotion Regulation	*Opposite to Emotion*
	Week 4: Interpersonal Effectiveness	*4 Horsemen of the Apocalypse*
Month 3	Week 1: Mindfulness	*Turtling*
	Week 2: Distress Tolerance	*Radical Acceptance*
	Week 3: Emotion Regulation	*ABC*
	Week 4: Interpersonal Effectiveness	*GIVE and FAST*

	Week 1: Mindfulness	*Nonjudgmental*
Month 4	Week 2: Distress Tolerance	*Half Smile*
	Week 3: Emotion Regulation	*MEDDSS*
	Week 4: Interpersonal Effectiveness	*DEAR SELF*

The second way to teach DBT skills in a group format is one that is spontaneous in nature. Here the clinician picks a skill based on the content of what the clients bring in for group that session. This is similar to the spontaneous option under Individual Session discussed previously. This method takes considerable knowledge of DBT and confidence on the part of the clinician.

Case Management Appointments

These appointments are typically focused on meeting basic needs, connecting with community resources and advocacy. DBT skills can be taught to clients to help them meet their own needs and to deal with frustration, setbacks and other difficulties. DBT skills can also empower clients to be effective in asking for help, maintaining housing, investing in healthy relationships, and engaging in meaningful activities—such as employment or service work. Case managers, social workers and other staff can introduce a skill, build motivation, practice the skill with the client and encourage the client to use the skill in their life.

Behavioral Health Consultations

These interventions occur in primary care offices and during other medical appointments. They are typically 15–20 minutes, and patients may meet with the behavioral health consultant once, sporadically, or on an ongoing basis. Because of this, behavioral health consultations may be one of the briefest ways to deliver DBT. In this setting, clients learn one or two skills, are given a handout and other resources, and are encouraged to practice using the skills. The skills may target improving physical health through improved nutrition, exercise and stress management; or improving mental health and wellness. Some patients only need a few skills and can make significant changes in their lives, while other patients will benefit from a referral to a mental health therapist for more in-depth work. Ideal skills for behavioral health consultations are *MEDDSS, Square Breathing, Moment to Pause, Mindful Eating, Self-Soothe Kit, Love Dandelions, Ride the Wave* and *Broken Record*.

Medication Management

Psychiatric prescribers and primary care physicians can teach and reinforce the use of DBT skills in addition to providing medication management. This can be done in collaboration with other clinicians or treatment teams, or it can be done independently if the client doesn't have additional contact with mental health staff. *MEDDSS*, in particular, is a fairly straightforward skill and is directly applicable to medical appointments.

Outreach Visits

Working with clients in their own environments provides great opportunities to facilitate their adoption of skills in their lives. Outreach clinicians can see the client's strengths and challenges firsthand. They can then choose the most appropriate skills and teach them in vivo, and clients can ask for help as they run into difficulties. Seeing how the client makes use of the idea of balance and implements the skills allows multiple opportunities for positive reinforcement. An example would be using *ACCEPTS* when a client is very upset about not getting what they want. An outreach worker could teach the skill of *Wise*

Mind when the client is out of balance with thinking or feeling, or the skill of *Willingness* when things are going badly for a client.

Recreation Activities

Having fun learning DBT skills makes it more likely that clients will use the skills in a variety of situations in their lives. Therefore, teaching and reinforcing these skills can be woven into various activities, such as games, arts and crafts, listening to music and sports. Particularly when working with teenagers, the clinician can access multiple media formats to reinforce learning, such as video games, music, movies and the internet.

When utilizing film, TV or music, clinicians can ask clients to look for examples of skills being used, and then have clients bring those examples into group or individual sessions. Another way to use TV or film is to identify a difficulty or conflict that a character is experiencing and then have the clients decide what skills would be useful for the character and why.

Arts and crafts are also a way clients can create representations of skills. For example, by drawing the path they're on and all the twists and turns their path has taken, clients can show how they use *Turning the Mind*. Other skills that can easily be turned into a craft project include *Ride the Wave, Lemonade* and *Turtling*.

Lastly, when clients play sports, clinicians can point out that they are often trying to be as *Effective* as much as possible. Likewise, not playing as well as desired or losing the game is an opportunity to use *Ride the Wave* or *Love Dandelions*.

Unstructured Time in the Therapeutic Community

This is one of the best opportunities to coach clients to use skills and provides many opportunities to reinforce skills. All staff and clients can learn the skills as they help one another use them; and it is this type of ongoing practice opportunity that will ensure clients' success when they return to their own environment full time. Staff and other clients can comment when they see a client using a skill, such as *DEAR SELF, Nonjudgmental* or *Self-Soothe Kit*. Additionally, asking the question "How can you use your skills?" reminds clients about their skills and gently holds them accountable for using them. Some of the examples from Recreational Activities can also be used here.

In the Classroom

Teachers and school counselors can weave DBT skills into their lesson plans. They can focus on teaching skills that will resonate with specific age groups, and they can teach them in developmentally-appropriate language. Using play therapy and expressive therapies along with DBT skills reinforces learning for children and teenagers; and a lot of repetition helps ensure that learning happens and that it will be transferred to home life. It is also very useful to orient family members to the skills (covered in the following section).

In addition to the suggestions in Recreational Activities and Unstructured Time in the Therapeutic Community, skills can be illustrated in stories. For example, *The Old Man and the Sea* by Ernest Hemingway contains several skills, including *Feeling Not Acting, Keeping It In Perspective* and *Half Smile*. Moments in history show the use of skills as well. For instance, the Industrial Revolution illustrates *Effectively* and *SPECIFIC PATHS*. Alexander Graham Bell used *Crisis Survival Network* when he called out for his assistant while inventing the telephone. These are only a few examples of the daily opportunities teachers have to illustrate DBT skills.

At Home with Family and Friends

When a client's family and friends learn DBT skills, it gives their family and friends the opportunity to apply the skills in their own lives and to appreciate how complex and challenging the skills are to use. In addition, their familiarity with the skills provides opportunities for coaching and positive reinforcement. Family and friends can ask the same questions as clinical staff, such as: "How did your skills help with this?" They can then give feedback if there is an opportunity to use the skill more effectively or say "Good job" when it is used well. For instance, when a client is having difficulty remembering to use *Nonjudgmental* with themselves or others, family and friends can gently remind the client and can help them overcome any barriers. Friends and family can also practice *Square Breathing, Opposite to Emotion* or *Turn the Tables* with the client, among other skills.

SETTINGS

DBT has been used to treat mental health, addictions and co-occurring disorders in a variety of settings across the country, including private practice, outpatient group practices or agencies, primary care offices, intensive outpatient or day treatment programs, as well as in residential or inpatient programs.

Below are some tips for using DBT in some of these settings:

Private practice:

- Don't be the client's only resource.

- Balance skills with the client's desire to process.

- Emphasize usefulness of skills for client needs.

- Assign homework and review regularly.

- Consider joining a consultation group.

Outpatient group practice or agency:

- Orient all team members to DBT.

- Have two or more clinicians implement the model.

- Connect the model with treatment philosophy and existing clinical practices.

- Set up implementation for success.

- Teach and review DBT in both individual and group sessions.

Primary care offices:

- Orient primary care physicians and nursing staff to the DBT framework.

- Have the healthcare team decide which skills are most applicable to their patients' most common needs.

- Develop mini skill sessions that can be delivered in 15- to 20-minute appointments.

- Document skills taught in patients' charts so medical staff can reinforce the use of skills.

- Develop diary cards unique to the primary care office.

- If patients have access to MyChart or similar electronic health records, they can email diary cards to the behavioral health consultants who are their health coaches.

- Refer out patients who need more intensive DBT services.

Intensive outpatient or day treatment programs:

- Train staff on the basics of DBT and have them use their skills at work.

- Create diary cards specific to the program.

- Reinforce learning in the milieu at every opportunity.

- Coach clients and team, and provide feedback regularly.

- Tie most or all clinical services to DBT.

- Use repetition and demonstration.

Residential and inpatient programs:

- All staff play an essential role.

- Milieu and support staff can coach and reinforce skills.

- Use expressive therapies.

- Weave DBT skills and philosophy into treatment philosophy.

- Have staff demonstrate skills.

- Have staff use skills to foster resilience in the workplace.

ADAPTING FOR DIVERSITY

As mentioned earlier, Pamela Hays (2007) created the ADDRESSING acronym for considering issues related to diversity when working with clients:

A = Age and Generation

D = Developmental Disabilities

D = Acquired Disabilities

R = Religion and Spirituality

E = Ethnicity

S = Socioeconomic Status

S = Sexual Orientation

I = Indigenous Heritage

N = National Origin

G = Gender

Age and Generation

Clients can be divided into four age groups: children, teenagers/young adults, adults and older adults. They can also be identified in terms of the generation to which they belong. These groups are discussed in more detail later in the chapter.

Developmental Disabilities

Adults with developmental disabilities, head trauma, low cognitive functioning or cognitive decline can benefit from DBT delivered in a simplified manner. Therefore, it's important to consider developmental variables when choosing skills for clients; and also when placing clients in an age-appropriate group. For instance, clients who have excelled developmentally may feel more at home with an older age group, whereas those who have exhibited problematic or impaired development may resonate more with a younger age group.

To assess for developmental disabilities, clinicians will want to determine whether the client met developmental milestones or developed more quickly or slowly than is typical, and if there are any diagnosed neurodevelopmental disorders. It is also important to note that not all developmental disabilities are immediately obvious in session.

Acquired Disabilities

In addition to developmental disabilities, clinicians must also screen for physical, cognitive, emotional or psychological disabilities and, if so, adapt how the skills are taught accordingly. Evaluate the client's deficits and strengths acquired throughout the lifespan, and consider the impact of any abuse, trauma or loss that may be present. Then choose skills to foster independence and resiliency, such as *Lemonade, MEDDSS, Nonjudgmental, GIVE* and *FAST.*

Religion and Spirituality

Be supportive and inclusive if the client has a religious or spiritual practice in their life, and minimize the impact of shame and guilt if present. Try to match values and beliefs with skills such as *SPECIFIC PATHS* and *Turtling.* For instance, turtles carry the world on their backs in the Hindu religion; and from this perspective, they have an extremely important role in maintaining balance. Tap into a community's support opportunities as well, if that is useful for the client.

Ethnicity

Individuals of differing races and ethnicities often exhibit unique cultural differences, including beliefs, rituals, holidays, values and relationships. When working with a variety of ethnic and racial groups, temper curiosity with respect; learn from the clients, and do any needed homework outside of the clinical process. In addition, be inclusive of values and worldviews. Don't underestimate either current or historical impacts of racism, discrimination and oppression. Be sure to also consider the specific ethnic community's perspective on mental health and substance use problems and the role of counseling. Some ethnic communities are supportive of counseling, while in other groups it is highly stigmatized. Suggested skills are *Self-Soothe Kit* and *Effectively.*

Socioeconomic Status

It is necessary for clinicians to consider the impact of poverty and privilege, given differences in wealth, lifestyle, social status and education among clients. Where indicated, help the client access resources to meet their basic needs. Evaluate lifestyle strengths and weaknesses, and empower clients to use skills to live more effectively. Additionally, consider how a client's socioeconomic status interacts with other aspects of diversity. Suggested skills are *Nonjudgmental* and *Keeping It In Perspective.*

Sexual Orientation

Clinicians must also consider a client's sexual orientation—who they are emotionally, physically and psychologically attracted to. This concept includes heterosexuality (attraction between people of different genders), as well as several other sexual orientations outlined in the following LGTBQQI acronym:

L = Lesbians are women who are emotionally, physically and/or psychologically attracted to other women.

G = The term "gay" can be used to refer to men or women who are emotionally, physically and/or psychologically attracted to individuals of the same gender.

T = Transgender individuals psychologically identify as a gender other than the sex assigned to them at birth.

B = Bisexual individuals are emotionally, physically and/or psychologically attracted to people of at least two gender identities.

Q = Queer is a term used to indicate any aspect of the LGBTQQI spectrum.

Q = Questioning individuals aren't sure of their sexual orientation or gender identity.

I = Intersex individuals have partial or a variety of primary and secondary sex characteristics.

When working with LGTBQQI clients, assess for internalized homophobia and psychological distress related to sexual orientation or gender identity. Assist with the "coming out" process where indicated, and connect clients who are members of a particular group with allies and community supports in their city and on the internet. Suggested skills are *Crisis Survival Network* and *Dealing with Difficult People*.

Indigenous Heritage

Another aspect for consideration is whether a client is of indigenous heritage. This can include Native Americans, Alaska Natives and any group that is indigenous to a specific geographic area. When working with these clients, make sure to integrate their values, worldview, perspective on health and healing, any connections to nature and the importance of their ancestors. This diversity component also tends to interact with religious or spiritual beliefs, ethnicity and socioeconomic status. When selecting skills based on this information, a clinician might choose *Turtling* because turtles are very important symbols to some Native American and other indigenous communities. Suggested skills are *Turtling* and *Half Smile*.

National Origin

Nationality can greatly impact clients who are immigrants or first-generation citizens. While this impact may be more historical in nature for clients whose families immigrated during previous generations, clinicians should nonetheless consider both current and historical factors. Pay attention to trauma that occurred in the home country, even if it didn't happen directly to the client. For example, a client of German heritage and Jewish descent may be affected by the Holocaust because their family members were imprisoned. Foster pride and tradition, as long as they don't lead to judgments against other groups. Also, evaluate discrepancies with the dominant culture for any stress that this may cause. Suggested skills are *Wise Mind* and *SPECIFIC PATHS*.

Gender

Gender identity refers to a person's psychological sense of their gender, and it may or may not correlate with the biological sex characteristics they were born with. Gender roles play an important part here as well, as clients will vary with regard to the typical expectations, activities and duties ascribed to different genders. Gender expression is the physical display of a person's gender identity; for example, the type of clothing and hairstyles a person chooses to wear. This category is quite dynamic with other diversity components. When teaching DBT skills, be sure to adapt metaphors and skills that are consistent with the client's gender identity, role and expression. Suggested skills are *DEAR SELF*, *GIVE* and *FAST*.

THE MIDDLE PATH

In addition to the four skills modules, DBT also focuses on the Middle Path. The Middle Path is a synthesis of dialectical thinking and behavior that concentrates on families learning balance and collaboration, instead of getting stuck in extremes. The Middle Path asks everyone involved in the family to metaphorically walk a mile in one another's shoes.

Families are taught to validate themselves and others in the family for their strengths and for what is going well. Parents are asked to focus on behavioral change, while not speculating on motives. Additionally, families are asked to have willingness to participate in DBT treatment, collaborate on solutions, implement DBT strategies, make sure everyone uses DBT skills in the family, and sustain the use of DBT strategies and skills for the long term.

The Middle Path believes modifying problematic behavior can be accomplished by:

- Observing and describing problematic behavior in nonjudgmental ways

- Encouraging *Opposite to Emotion* or another skill

- Coaching the client to use skills effectively

- Educating the client to notice problematic behaviors and triggers early and to self-regulate

- Visualizing or in vivo practice of changing behaviors and using skills

- Planning to deal with obstacles and barriers to identifying problem behavior and using skills

Additionally, the Middle Path helps families find balance, particularly in terms of:

- Providing discipline and structure along with fun and relaxation

- Providing oversight of the children along with increased opportunities for age-appropriate independence

- Fostering healthy interdependence

- Communicating effectively and maintaining healthy boundaries

Since most teenagers and many young adults live with, or are in regular contact with their families, we want to involve the family in the treatment process whenever possible. However, this is sometimes not possible, or it is contraindicated. In these cases, involving other support individuals in the Middle Path components of treatment is an option. A very useful resource on the Middle Path is *Dialectical Behavior Therapy with Suicidal Adolescents* by Alec Miller (2017).

Parenting

Parents can use DBT strategies and skills with children and adolescents. Sometimes youth create their own problems, sometimes they contribute to their problems and sometimes problems happen to them. Regardless, they still need to figure out how to deal with problems, minimize their negative impact and strategize how to avoid similar problems in the future. It is important for parents to remember that youth are doing the best they can, that they need to be more effective, and that they are responsible for dealing with their problems even when it isn't their fault. Maintaining this stance can assist parents in having compassion for, and an ability to support, their children while holding them accountable to be effective, prosocial and healthy.

DBT views reality as subjective and maintains that there is no one, single truth. It is very helpful to remember this framework when interacting with youth. Families can agree to disagree sometimes, while parents maintain authority and set the rules. Likewise, family members can suspend the need to be right at times, while appreciating multiple perspectives. Because everyone's experience is real for them, it is important to avoid making assumptions and to instead validate the youth's reality. After all, the world is very different for youth now than it was when parents were growing up. Parents can be curious about what is happening for their child, explore their thinking and feelings and provide validation. Through all of this, parents should also maintain a self-awareness of the thoughts, feelings, communications and behaviors they are experiencing.

STRATEGIES FOR PARENTS

Although there is no perfect solution when parenting, some effective parental strategies include: assume that children's motives are well-intentioned, avoid jumping to worst-case scenarios and develop priorities for what needs to be addressed first. In this process, parents are encouraged to remember what they have control over and when it is more effective to let go—sometimes parents have to pick the battles they choose to engage in. Parents will benefit from knowing their child's warning signs and vulnerabilities so they can respond early and effectively.

Additionally, having multiple strategies is more effective than using the same strategy that worked before. Parents can balance validation while applying consequences, and they can also focus on their child's behavior while being *Nonjudgmental*. Additionally, parents will be more effective if they stay in the here-and-now while avoiding problems of the past and concerns of the future; and if they can deal with all the demands of being a parent while focusing on one thing at a time.

Sometimes unintentional invalidation happens, even among well-meaning parents. This can occur when parents tell their children that in the big picture something doesn't matter, if other kids were really their friends then they wouldn't treat them that way or they don't know what stress is. While parents may be well-intentioned with these types of messages, the youth may still experience them as painful invalidations. Parents are encouraged to minimize unintentional invalidation by being *Nonjudgmental* and not defining their children based on their behavior. Parents should avoid assigning feelings or thoughts, while also not placating the youth. The youth's experience is reality for them. Parents can share their emotions and thoughts, while demonstrating how to be upset or in pain, and still be effective in the process.

Parents may also need to be reminded of the importance of self-care. Many parents think they have to take care of their children first and themselves second. However, if parents give all of themselves away, then there is nothing left, and they can't properly take care of their children or themselves. Self-care helps parents recharge and instills resiliency. Part of self-care is helping parents to be dialectical, engage in mindfulness, tolerate distress, regulate emotions, and be effective in relationships. Therefore, parents can use a variety of DBT skills to engage in appropriate self-care. One powerful skill for parents is *Moment to Pause*, which teaches parents to take a deep breath, check in with themselves and the situation, become more responsive and less reactive and do what works. Additional skills include *Self-Soothe Kit, Willingness, Keeping It In Perspective, Half Smile, ABC, Broken Record* and *Repairs*.

Parents can also benefit from leveraging naturally occurring resources so they don't feel like they have to do all the parenting on their own and they can sometimes get a break. Naturally occurring resources are community resources that are typically available regardless of the economy, such as teachers, school programs, healthy family and friends, libraries, parks and recreation and youth programs.

Strategies for Children

School-age children and pre-teens can also benefit from learning and using DBT in their lives. In addition, with appropriate modifications, it is even possible to conduct DBT with children ages 4–13. To effectively use DBT with children, it is first necessary to simplify and shorten it.

- **Mindfulness** can be broken down by teaching kids to be in the here-and-now. Children learn that mindfulness is about focusing on what is happening right now—not earlier in the day or yesterday, or worrying about later or tomorrow. Instead of calling it mindfulness, it can be referred to as "paying attention to right now."

- **Distress Tolerance** can also be useful for kids by helping them learn that they can manage their behaviors and frustration levels. Distress Tolerance can also be referred to as "how to deal with being frustrated."

- Similarly, **Emotion Regulation** can be applied by teaching kids about their feelings and how to manage them. There are many tools to help kids learn about their emotions, including posters of different facial expressions and educational videos on emotions. Emotion Regulation can be referred to as "getting to know your feelings."

- Lastly, **Interpersonal Effectiveness**—or having effective relationships with family members, friends and others—can help kids learn how to maintain healthy relationships with their friends, family and teachers. Interpersonal Effectiveness can be referred to as "how to play well with others."

Modification of basic DBT skills can foster healthy development and lay the foundation for a skillful life trajectory. The younger the child, the fewer skills should be used. In general, when teaching DBT skills to children, it is important to use developmentally-appropriate language, concrete concepts, lots of repetition, demonstration of skills and play therapy techniques. It is essential to get the family involved as well, by having them practice the skills with the child at home. If possible, it is also preferable to even involve teachers, daycare workers and anyone who interacts with the child on a regular basis. All of these individuals can provide encouragement and reinforcement. The more the child uses the skills and gets feedback from the environment, the more skillful the child will become.

For children between four and six years old, two or three simple skills are recommended. Skills that can be used with this age group are *Moment to Pause, Self-Soothe Kit* and *Repairs. Moment to Pause* is similar to taking a time out—it helps the child to stop and think things through. *Self-Soothe Kit* helps children deal with frustration and upset by using things that are soothing—such as a stuffed animal, toy car or special blanket. The *Repairs* skill teaches children to apologize, and also accept when someone else apologizes.

For children ages seven to nine, the above skills can be useful, as well as additional skills: *Feeling Not Acting, Lemonade* and *Turtling.* For example, children can learn impulse control through the *Feeling Not Acting* skill, which teaches them that they can feel strong emotions and impulses without acting on them. Similarly, the *Lemonade* skill teaches children to redirect weaknesses and turn them into strengths. With this skill, children learn to take behaviors that get them in trouble and use them differently so that they become strengths.

For instance, if a child does not listen in class or at home because they are drawing, their artistic ability and creativity can be channeled in appropriate ways that increase the child's self-esteem and self-efficacy. At the same time, the child can learn appropriate behavior for class and family activities. Finally, *Turtling* teaches children to use a variety of strategies to take care of themselves just like turtles do; and when life turns the children upside down, they can also be self-righting—even if it takes a while and a lot of energy.

Additional skills that are useful for pre-teens include *Turning the Mind, Crisis Survival Network* and *Ride the Wave. Turning the Mind* teaches children that they are in the driver's seat with their thinking, feeling and behavior. They can continue to drive down the problematic road of delinquency or other problematic behaviors, or they can make the choice to change roads toward a more effective path. This is an empowering skill that resonates with many pre-teens. Many children look forward to getting their driver's license, and they feel free and like adults when they finally do get their licenses. This skill taps into this idea. Children learn that they are in the driver's seat of their lives, and they can decide where they go.

Of course, there will also be roadblocks and unforeseen difficulties that they will need to learn how to navigate in order to keep driving. *Crisis Survival Network* is about having friends, family and mentors with whom the child can connect to get support, feedback and advice. *Ride the Wave* is learning to tolerate problematic impulses, painful emotions and difficult situations until they naturally subside. A very useful metaphor for this skill involves harnessing the energy from these impulses, emotions or situations to creatively surf. In doing so, children learn that they can surf the wave and have fun instead of being destructive.

Some other skills that can be modified to work with children are *Half Smile, Broken Record*, and *4 Horsemen of the Apocalypse. Half Smile* teaches children in the middle of frustrations or difficulties to find anything in their lives to have a tiny smile about. When they are smiling a little bit, they are less tense; and smiling also tells their brains that they are experiencing pleasure and happiness, which changes the brains' chemistry and improves moods. *Broken Record* teaches children to repeatedly remind themselves of who they want to be and the kind of life they want to have, and then act consistently with that. Lastly, the *4 Horsemen of the Apocalypse* skill teaches children to identify the most destructive behaviors they exhibit in relationships and then figure out how to engage in fewer of these behaviors.

For example, when children spend hours playing video games, this can be a "horseman" with regard to their relationships with their parents. By learning this skill, children can develop strategies to play video games while also investing in activities with their parents, and getting homework and chores completed.

Teaching Tips

When teaching these skills to children, it is recommended that a variety of strategies be used. This can include visual cues, such as stop signs to remind children to use their *Moment to Pause* skill. Video and TV examples can also serve as effective strategies. For instance, *Turtling* can be combined with watching cartoons or movies about the *Teenage Mutant Ninja Turtles*. Similarly, skills such as *Feeling Not Acting* and *Half Smile* can be used while playing games. Play-acting and role-plays can be used when practicing *4 Horsemen of the Apocalypse* and *Crisis Survival Network*.

In addition, *Repairs* can be demonstrated in play therapy by fixing something and then talking about how to fix friendships. Kinesthetic activities can be used to demonstrate how to make *Lemonade* and use *Broken Record*. Artwork can also be used to demonstrate *Ride the Wave* and *Turning the Mind* by having children draw themselves doing each of these activities. Child therapists can use many of their typical techniques to teach and reinforce children using DBT skills as well.

Another area of modification for children involves simplifying the format of diary cards, as adult diary cards are too complex for children to use. An alternative is to use a monthly calendar template involving stickers. Each day that the child uses a skill, they put a sticker on the calendar for that day. This approach gives immediate feedback to the child and the family that the skills are being used. If the child is old enough, the next step can involve putting a sticker on the calendar for each day that they use two skills, and then only putting stickers on days when at least three skills are used. Parents, primary caregivers, teachers and other important adults in the child's life can watch for skills being used and let the child know when it looks like they are using a skill. These same adults can remind the child to use their skills and encourage the use of more and more skills.

Chain analysis is a complex process that helps the clinician and client identify the chain of events that led up to the problem behavior. By analyzing the chain of events, adult clients learn how they could have used their skills at each link in the chain of events. However, the process of completing a chain analysis can be too complex for many clients and even clinicians to understand, and it would clearly not work for children.

An alternative to helping children conduct chain analysis is to use plastic chain links—a common toy that can be easily found at stores or online—or to create paper chain links using construction paper. The children can talk about how each link is the next thing that happened that led to their problem behavior, such as a temper tantrum, getting into a fight, running away, or being disruptive.

Sometime after the problem behavior has stopped and the child is able to talk about it, take out the plastic chain. Start with one link, and talk about the problem behavior. Then take another link and ask the child what happened just before the problem behavior. Add that link to the first link. Then ask the child which skill could they have used to avoid the problem behavior. Next, take another link, and ask the child what happened before the last link. Add that link to the chain. Again, discuss what skills could have been used to stop the process. Depending on the age of the child and their ability to understand this activity, another two or three links can be used.

A different way to get at this concept is to use a stoplight. Red represents the problem behavior, yellow represents the warning signs leading up to the problem behavior, and green represents what set the child on the road to the problem behavior.

For children to get the maximum benefit out of learning DBT skills, it is essential that family members also learn and use their DBT skills. The gains that children make from DBT will be cemented and sustained over time if the family also practices DBT. When everyone in the family uses these skills, it also supports the overall health and increased level of functioning of the family.

STRATEGIES FOR TEENAGERS

DBT can also be used effectively with teenagers and young adults to target behaviors such as delinquency, substance use, violence, or other acting-out behaviors. Although it may be the treatment of choice for individuals who are displaying traits of BPD and/or engaging in self-harm behaviors, DBT can be used with a variety of diagnoses such as oppositional defiant disorder, conduct disorder, depression, bipolar, anxiety, trauma and attention deficit disorder. DBT can also be used as a strengths-based program, by providing non-behaviorally-challenged teenagers with useful life skills to foster healthy development, and to prevent future difficulties and problems.

When implementing DBT with teenagers, the skills modules should be adapted accordingly.

- **Mindfulness** needs to be taught in a more active manner with teenagers and young adults, which can be accomplished through mindful movement with walking, yoga and tai chi. Mindfulness can also be practiced during creative activities, such as listening to and playing music or engaging in artistic endeavors.

- **Distress Tolerance** is very useful for these clients since it teaches them how to deal with stress and difficulties by building frustration tolerance.

- **Emotion Regulation** is also right on target for the adolescent developmental milestones. By teaching these clients how to effectively manage their emotions and control their impulses, Emotion Regulation provides the building blocks for successful self-management.

- Teenagers and young adults are also very invested in friendships and romantic relationships, so they will benefit enormously from **Interpersonal Effectiveness**.

- Some skills that appeal to, and are useful for, teenagers and young adults are: *Turtling, Wise Mind, Square Breathing, Moment to Pause, Effectively, Willingness, Half Smile, Turning the Mind, Self-Soothe Kit, Crisis Survival Network, Opposite to Emotion, Lemonade, Ride the Wave, ACCEPTS or IMPROVE, ABC, 4 Horsemen of the Apocalypse, Repairs, GIVE, FAST* and *DEAR SELF*.

Teaching Tips

Because teenagers and young adults have rapidly developing brains, they are often able to learn things very quickly. However, it is possible that clients in this age group can learn several skills and demonstrate an understanding of these skills, without necessarily using the skills in their lives. For this reason, it is recommended that teenagers be asked to demonstrate the ways that they use skills in their daily lives and to discuss in detail what was useful or not useful about the skills.

Teenagers and young adults are more likely to engage in the therapy process if it feels less like therapy to them. This can be accomplished by making therapy interesting and fun. Providing a variety of activities and using multimedia is highly recommended to accomplish this.

Using various forms of multimedia, such as TV, music and the internet, goes a long way toward engaging teens and young adults. Because teenagers and young adults are enormously connected with technology, clinicians who can demonstrate an understanding of the current technology and subject matter in songs, video games, movies, TV and internet stories will gain credibility with these clients and help them connect what they are learning in DBT with examples pertinent to their lives. For instance, video clips from TV shows or movies can be shown in a group format or an individual session, followed by a discussion about what DBT skills the characters were using and how those skills worked for them.

Music is also very important to this age group. In popular music, there are many examples of songs that demonstrate skill use, including:

- *ABC*: "Best Day of My Life," American Authors
- *Broken Record*: "Love Yourself," Justin Bieber, "Gotta Be Somebody," Nickelback
- *Crisis Survival Network*: "1-800-273-8255," Logic
- *DEAR SELF:* "Sweet Escape," Gwen Stefani
- *Dealing With Difficult People*: "Bad Blood," Taylor Swift
- *Dialectics*: "Harmony Hall," Vampire Weekend
- *FAST*: "Shake It Off," Taylor Swift, "Big Girls Don't Cry," Fergie
- *GIVE*: "Humble and Kind," Tim McGraw, "Be Without You," Mary J. Blige
- *Half Smile*: "There's Hope," India Arie, "Smile," Uncle Kracker
- *IMPROVE:* "Take Me Away," Natasha Bedingfield

- *Keeping It In Perspective*: "Titanium," Sia
- *Mindfulness*: "Right Now," Akon
- *ONE MIND*: "Living In The Moment," Jason Mraz
- *Opposite To Emotions*: "Rainbow," Ke$ha
- *Radical Acceptance:* "Not Ready to Make Nice," Dixie Chicks
- *Repairs*: "Sorry," Buckcherry, "Just Give Me A Reason," P!nk,
- *SPECIFIC PATHS:* "Listen," Beyonce
- *Turning The Mind*: "Dead & Gone," TI & JT, "Happy," Pharrell Williams

With the use of a laptop, videos for these songs can be watched in session and then discussed. Another way to include music is to print out the lyric sheets, and read and discuss the lyrics in session. Once the clients see that there are examples of skills in music that they listen to, they can look for their own examples, which they can then teach their therapist and other clients.

When conducting DBT with teenagers and young adults, another important area of modification involves diary cards. Given that traditional diary cards keep track of skill use via numbers, it is highly likely that teenagers and young adults will wait until shortly before their therapy session to fill out their cards. This reduces the usefulness of the diary cards. To avoid this, it is recommended that teenagers and young adults count the number of times they use their skills daily and then write out what happened in narrative form:

- Examples of when the skills were used
- Ways the skills were useful
- Barriers to using the skills and how they can overcome them

Increasing the use of skills can also be accomplished by using incentives or rewards to encourage teenagers and young adults to use their DBT skills. This can include a point system, award certificates, "DBT bucks," token economies and special privileges—to name just a few. Teenagers and young adults will make use of DBT if they see that it is beneficial for them and if the process is fun, interesting and engaging.

PROVIDING DBT TO ADULTS AND OLDER ADULTS

Adults

Over the last 25 years, DBT has been expanded for use with adults who have a variety of presenting problems, diagnoses and strengths. Indeed, the majority of this text is about using DBT with adults. It is also worth mentioning that when encouraging adult clients to use DBT skills, their motivation, goals and values should be part of the treatment process.

As mentioned in Chapter 2, it is essential to consider the client's Stage of Change about their presenting problem, engaging in DBT, and using DBT skills. While clinicians may be in the *action* stage, clients are often in the *pre-contemplation* or *contemplation* stage. If your client is in one of those stages, it is too soon to introduce new skills or to have expectations that the client will make significant changes. Instead of trying to persuade or force change, use validation strategies.

Additionally, listen for clients talking about how they are being skillful. They may be using all or part of a DBT skill without even knowing it. In these situations, label the skill or partial skill being used, highlight how it worked for the client, provide lots of positive reinforcement and encourage the client to continue to use the skill as much as possible. This strategy increases buy-in and may help the clients move to the *action* Stage of Change. Once clients are in late *preparation* or *action*, then new skills can be taught.

Motivation is also an important consideration. Motivation is often about self-interest—what's in it for the individual. Everyone has self-interest, which can be healthy and functional when balanced with the interests of others. Consistent with DBT's focus on building a life worth living, clinicians support self-interest that is prosocial and respectful of others. It is important to consider questions to help identify the client's self-interest and motivation. What is important to the client? What are their values? Who do they want to be? What do they want to accomplish? Asking these questions can help the clinician consider what would motivate the client to make changes and use new skills. Tapping into how the client will benefit highlights the reason for working hard, trying something new and staying the course with change even when it doesn't seem to be working.

Another consideration when working with adults, as well as other age groups, is developmental stages and tasks. According to Erik and Joan Erikson (1997), the following represents some of the different stages of psychosocial development:

Age Group	Development Tasks	Central Process	Psychosocial Crisis	Core Pathology	Adaptive Ego Quality
Late Adolescence (18–24)	• Autonomy from parents • Gender identity • Internalized morality • Career choice	Role experimentation	Individual identity vs. identity confusion	Repudiation	Fidelity to values
Early Adulthood (25–34)	• Exploring intimate relationships • Childbearing • Work • Lifestyle	Mutuality among peers	Intimacy vs. isolation	Exclusivity	Love
Middle Adulthood (35–60)	• Managing a career • Nurturing significant relationships • Expanding caring relationships • Managing the household	Person-environment fit and creativity	Generativity vs. stagnation	Rejectivity	Care

Erikson & Erikson, 1997

Clinicians can use this framework to determine what stage the client is in and how they are doing with developmental tasks and central processes. DBT interventions and skills can then be chosen to facilitate the adaptive ego quality for the client's stage of development.

For example, a client in the Early Adulthood stage who is working on having a family and balancing career aspirations could benefit from maintaining a dialectical balance between self and others, as well as between career and family. Skills that might be useful in this stage are *Effectively, Half Smile, MEDDSS* and *Broken Record.* Clients in the Middle Adulthood stage who are working on nurturing relationships and maintaining a household could benefit from maintaining a dialectical balance between independence and codependence, as well as between wants and needs. Skills that might be useful in this stage are *ONE MIND, Willingness, Ride the Wave* and *Repairs.*

In addition to developmental considerations, it is also useful to contemplate clients' needs. Although Maslow's hierarchy of needs provides a common conceptualization of human needs, Manfred A. Max-Neef proposed an alternative taxonomy of fundamental human needs and theory of human scale development.

Need	Being (qualities)	Having (things)	Doing (actions)	Interacting (settings)	DBT skills to help satisfy this need
Subsistence	physical and mental health	food, shelter, work	feed, clothe, rest, work	living environment, social setting	*MEDDSS* or *ABC*
Protection	care, adaptability, autonomy	social security, health systems, work	cooperate, plan, take care of, help	social environment, dwelling	*DEAR SELF* or *Lemonade*
Affection	respect, sense of humor, generosity, sensuality	friendships, family, relationships with nature	share, take care of, express emotions	privacy, intimate spaces of togetherness	*GIVE* or *Crisis Survival Network*
Understanding	critical capacity, curiosity, intuition	literature, teachers, policies, education	analyze, study, meditate, investigate	schools, families, universities, communities	*Wise Mind* or *Opposite to Emotion*
Participation	receptiveness, dedication, sense of humor	responsibilities, duties, work, rights	cooperate, dissent, express opinions	associations, parties, churches, neighborhoods	*Observe, Describe & Participate*
Leisure	imagination, tranquility, spontaneity	games, parties, peace of mind	daydream, remember, relax, have fun	landscapes, intimate spaces, places to be alone	*Self-Soothe Kit* or *Turn the Tables*
Creation	imagination, boldness, inventiveness, curiosity	abilities, skills, work, techniques	invent, build, design, work, compose, interpret	spaces for expression, workshops, audiences	*Keeping It In Perspective* or *Love Dandelions*
Identity	sense of belonging, self-esteem, consistency	language, religions, work, customs, values, norms	get to know oneself, grow, commit oneself	places one belongs to, everyday settings	*FAST* or *SPECIFIC PATHS*
Freedom	autonomy, passion, self-esteem, open-mindedness	equal rights	dissent, choose, run risks, develop awareness	anywhere	*Radical Acceptance* or *Relationship Mindfulness*

Max-Neef, 1989

Older Adults

Depending on which source you consult, older adulthood begins somewhere between 55 and 68 years of age. When working with older adults, it is important to assess their level of functioning, cognitive skills or stage of cognitive decline, physical energy and mobility and life history (such as their life course and historical events that they have lived through), and to modify DBT for these accordingly. Some older adults are also living with chronic diseases, the effects of which must also be factored into treatment. Suggested skills are *Observe, Describe & Participate, Radical Acceptance, Love Dandelions* and *Repairs.*

Some of the information and strategies discussed in the previous section on Adults are useful with older adults as well. Often these clients have many strengths and skills, so supporting and encouraging these is a useful strategy. Additionally, as older adults experience changes, such as retirement or physical decline, new skills may be indicated. When conducting DBT with older adults, it may be helpful to reference the older adult developmental stages in Erikson's stages of psychosocial development:

Age Group	Development Tasks	Central Process	Psychosocial Crisis	Core Pathology	Adaptive Ego Quality
Later Adulthood (61–75)	• Promoting intellectual vigor • Redirecting energy toward new roles • Accepting one's life • Developing a point of view on death	Introspection	Integrity vs. despair	Disdain	Wisdom
Old Age (76 until death)	• Coping with the physical changes of aging • Developing a psycho-historical perspective • Traveling through uncharted terrain	Social support	Immortality vs. extinction	Diffidence	Confidence

Erikson & Erikson, 1997

A client in the Later Adulthood stage who is working on adapting to new roles could benefit from maintaining a dialectical balance between the past and future, as well as between their existing strengths and new abilities. Skills that might be useful in this stage are *Turtling, Radical Acceptance, Lemonade* and *Relationship Assumptions.* Clients in the Old Age stage who are working on coping with aging can benefit from balancing accomplishments and loss of functioning, as well as appreciating life while preparing for the end. Skills that might be useful in this stage are *Be Mindful, Half Smile, ABC* and *Dealing with Difficult People.*

ADAPTING DBT TO YOUR PRACTICE

There are many ways DBT can be used. It is a complex model with many layers. Comprehensive DBT practiced with fidelity or adherence to the research protocol is one option for delivering DBT. However, for the creative clinician, DBT can also be adapted to work in a variety of settings, and with various client groups.

This chapter has provided several ideas on how to adapt and modify DBT. Use these ideas if they work for your clinical practice, or use them as a starting point to create your DBT protocols. Learn from the wisdom of clients, as they often have many examples of how DBT works for them, consult with your colleagues, and continue to read about DBT. Just as psychodynamic, humanistic therapy and CBT have continued to evolve over decades, DBT will continue to be adapted and modified to meet the changing needs of clients, communities and clinicians.

Chapter 6
Clinical Presentations

While DBT was created and well researched with BPD, it can be used with a variety of other diagnoses and clinical syndromes. Here are a few examples:

- Attentional Problems
- Anger and Emotion Dysregulation
- Bipolar Disorder
- Depression
- Grief and Loss
- Inadequate Stress Management
- Oppositional Defiant Disorder
- Substance Use Disorders: Mild and Severe
- Adjustment Disorder
- Anxiety Disorders
- Conduct Disorder
- Eating Disorders
- Impulse Control Problems
- Low Self-Esteem
- Relational Problems
- Trauma: Single and Complex

When conducting DBT with clients with varying clinical presentations, it is important to consider the following five components:

1. The benefits of being dialectical
2. How the skills modules (or categories) are useful
3. Recommendations for specific skills
4. Encourage the use of diary cards
5. Provide lots of opportunities for chain analysis

One of the benefits of being dialectical includes having a both/and perspective that empowers clients to take better care of themselves and establish an optimal level of functioning. Having a both/and perspective is the opposite of having an either/or, black-or-white, perfection-or-failure, with-me-or-against-me perspective. In the clinical presentations that follow, common dialectics will be identified along with a skill that will help facilitate achieving balance with the dialectic.

Before choosing specific skills, it is helpful to think through how each of the four DBT modules (Mindfulness, Distress Tolerance, Emotion Regulation and Interpersonal Effectiveness) will be useful for the client. These four areas can help in the following ways:

1. **Mindfulness** helps clients be in the here-and-now, stop ruminating about the past and reduce catastrophizing about the future.

2. **Distress Tolerance** helps clients learn frustration tolerance and how to deal with stress effectively.

3. **Emotion Regulation** provides clients with tools to engage in healthy emotional coping on a day-to-day basis.

4. **Interpersonal Effectiveness** empowers clients to be assertive, set appropriate boundaries and establish healthy self-respect, while investing in safe relationships.

Once the clinician has discussed the benefits of being dialectical and the usefulness of the four modules, specific skills can be chosen and taught to clients in session. Diary cards allow clients to evaluate what their problematic urges, feelings and behaviors are. Clients can then track the skills they used to effectively manage these problematic urges, feelings and behaviors. When a client engages in problematic behavior, they can also use chain analysis to see how using skills might have led to reductions in, or elimination of, the problem behavior.

In the presentations that follow, recommendations will be made for specific skills that can be used for each diagnosis or clinical syndrome. These are just suggestions, and clinicians can mix and match skills based on their style, practice setting and the needs of the client. However, there are a few skills that are useful for nearly all clients—*MEDDSS, Crisis Survival Network, Nonjudgmental* and *Effectively*—and it is recommended that most clients engaged in DBT learn these skills and use them on a regular basis.

MEDDSS provides a framework for self-care, and clients can practice *MEDDSS* every day—just like they take their vitamins or have a morning cup of coffee. With this skill, clients can do one or two things over which they have Mastery; spend a few minutes Exercising, such as walking around the block or stretching; be thoughtful about their Diet; take prescription Drugs as directed and not use illicit drugs; get a healthy amount of Sleep; and have a moment of Spirituality, connection or meaning.

Crisis Survival Network is another useful skill for most clients, which involves creating a list of family and friends who support the client. Clients are encouraged to use the list flexibly by including many people on this list—not just one or two individuals—as well as community support groups. Clients can then access their network when they are having a stressful day or are in a crisis.

The *Nonjudgmental* skill is about not assigning a value to oneself or others. Many clients have some negative core beliefs, including that they are damaged, unlovable and deserve to be unhappy. These beliefs fuel their unhealthy behavior. If clients can learn to suspend these core beliefs and other judgments, they can stop the unhealthy behavior and be more effective in their lives.

Finally, the *Effectively* skill is about doing what works. Clients work toward being more effective by identifying what works in a given situation, as opposed to focusing on what is right, wrong, fair or unfair. This allows clients to identify behavior that is less effective or ineffective, and then develop strategies to become more effective. Being effective is strengths-based and forgiving. If clients are ineffective one day, they can work on being more effective the next day.

It's important to remember that there are many ways to use DBT. Sometimes clients reject the skills offered and the clinician offers other skills. Every now and then a client doesn't like any of the skills offered and they create their own. DBT can be used as a flexible framework that is designed to help clients be more skillful and build a life worth living; it is important to meet clients where they are at and work to everyone's strengths. For all these reasons, we believe it is essential to be flexible, creative, curious, and aware of fallibility when using DBT with any client.

PRACTICE VIGNETTES

In order to continue to help reinforce what you have learned about DBT and give you an opportunity to practice it, we have developed vignettes for a variety of presenting problems. On the following pages are examples of the skills we might use for each presenting problem; however, these are simply ideas for starting points. Use these vignettes to think about how and when you might teach certain skills and omit others. There is a journaling opportunity for your own suggested skills and for you to describe how you would teach them to the particular client being described.

These exercises will help you in the future, when encountering a client with similar skill needs, because you will have a reference for ideas on presenting the skill(s) to the client. Most importantly, this will help you practice what you have been learning. You may wish to create a consultation group with others who are learning DBT and share your vignette ideas to get feedback and additional inspiration for methods of teaching the skills.

ATTENTIONAL PROBLEMS

Clients with ADHD and other attentional problems exhibit an inability to sustain attention, fail to complete tasks, exhibit high amounts of distractibility and quickly become bored. These clients often have a lot of energy and may learn best kinesthetically.

Dialectics

- Staying focused while one's mind wanders. Suggested skill: *Keeping It In Perspective*

- Completing tasks even when it is boring. Suggested skill: *Wise Mind*

- Knowing when multitasking is useful and when one thing at a time is more effective. Suggested skill: *Be Mindful*

Mindfulness helps these individuals remember to stay in the here-and-now, and not get distracted by other things. Being mindful increases attentional capacity. It is also helpful to be mindful when being distracted or multitasking, knowing that not everything has one's full attention or that others might be frustrated.

Distress Tolerance includes being able to tolerate and manage distress well, which will decrease the desire to be distracted or to move onto other things too quickly.

Emotion Regulation enables clients to effectively manage emotions; and having impulse control will reduce distractibility.

Interpersonal Effectiveness is realizing that distractions and tangents are frustrating for others. These individuals will benefit from making additional efforts to stay focused during interactions and social activities.

Attentional Problems
Practice Vignette

A 12-year-old cisgender female client has been enrolled in individual therapy for the last two months. The client has a lot of energy, is fidgety and switches conversation topics quickly. She is receiving Cs and Ds in school even though her IQ is above average. Primary caregivers express frustration because she starts her chores but often doesn't finish them. She enjoys gymnastics and painting.

Suggested Skills

- **Meta Skills:** *Effectively* will help her to focus on being as effective as she can be in her tasks, interactions and relationships, which will help her prioritize what is most important or needs to be dealt with first. *Nonjudgmental* will help her reduce negative judgments about herself when she gets frustrated, distracted and is unable to complete tasks.

- **Secondary Skills:** *Moment to Pause* will help her be more present with her internal and external experiences while also being more responsive and less reactive. She can also benefit from the *Lemonade* skill, which would use her energy and distractibility to engage in complex activities, multitask effectively and explore her creativity.

- **Ancillary Skill:** She can use the *ABC* skill by accumulating positives of when she has effectively managed her symptoms, building mastery by learning effective strategies to manage her symptoms and coping ahead with particularly challenging times and situations.

List other skills with your reasoning/purpose for selecting them for the client, and how you would teach these skills to the client:

_____

_____

_____

_____

_____

_____

_____

_____

ADJUSTMENT DISORDER

Adjustment disorder involves the development of emotional or behavioral symptoms in response to a stressor or major life change. Adjustment disorder can also be accompanied by anxiety, depression or both. This disorder tends to be milder than other mental health disorders and typically lasts less than six months.

Dialectics

- Dealing with stress while being able to enjoy life. Suggested skill: *Be Mindful*

- Managing problems while getting things done. Suggested skill: *Ride the Wave*

- Taking care of oneself while investing in relationships with others. Suggested skill: *Broken Record*

Mindfulness helps these individuals stay grounded in the here-and-now. Because the past is the past, and the future is not here yet, the only thing individuals have an influence over is the present moment. They can effectively deal with problems, stressors and changes right now by being solution-focused.

Distress Tolerance assists with lowering the stress and frustration individuals experience when adjusting to their changing circumstances.

Emotion Regulation helps individuals with adjustment disorder deal with the upheaval associated with life changes.

Interpersonal Effectiveness assists clients with effectively accessing support from friends and family as they go through troubled times.

Adjustment Disorder
Practice Vignette

A 21-year-old cisgender male, dealing with parental divorce and expulsion from college due to failing many courses, is experiencing sadness and anxiety. The client describes feeling immobilized and unable to make decisions. Sleeping and eating are impaired; however, there are no risk concerns and no use of drugs or alcohol. The client reports having supportive friends, and also states that he enjoys working on mechanical things like cars and appliances.

Suggested Skills

- **Meta Skills:** This client can use the *MEDDSS* skill to maintain structure in his life while ensuring that he is engaging in effective self-care strategies. Additionally, *Wise Mind* will help him balance uncomfortable feelings by thinking about his strengths and finding ways to manage his feelings.

- **Secondary Skills:** The *Opposite to Emotion* skill will help him combat the sadness and anxiety by engaging in activities that help him feel happy and relaxed. In addition, he can use *Turtling* by leveraging a variety of strategies to cope and manage his life.

- **Ancillary Skill:** The client can use *Willingness* to accept the reality of his situation, be empowered to work with his reality and avoid anything that might make it worse or more stressful.

List other skills with your reasoning/purpose for selecting them for the client, and how you would teach these skills to the client:

_____

_____

_____

_____

_____

_____

_____

_____

_____

ANGER AND EMOTION DYSREGULATION

Individuals with anger and emotion dysregulation exhibit extreme, often uncontrollable expressions of anger or other emotional responses that are disproportionate to the situation at hand. These responses often damage relationships, occupational pursuits and property, and can lead to long-term consequences—some of which may be legal in nature.

Dialectics

- Having intense emotions and wanting to be calm. Suggested skill: *Square Breathing*

- Feeling out of control and wanting to be in control. Suggested skill: *Moment to Pause*

- Having quick reactions while learning to be responsive. Suggested skill: *Feeling Not Acting*

Mindfulness helps clients to be in the moment, which empowers them to notice and intervene when they start to gear up emotionally.

Distress Tolerance teaches clients to manage and tolerate strong emotions and crises without acting out.

Emotion Regulation helps clients to maintain an awareness of their emotional state and pause for a moment, allowing them to focus on using a skill instead of acting out their emotions or impulses.

Interpersonal Effectiveness encourages clients to be effective in their relationships. This can help clients to avoid harming others emotionally or physically because it would damage their relationships; or if they get sufficient support from their relationships they don't have impulses to engage in problematic behavior.

Anger and Emotion Dysregulation
Practice Vignette

A 42-year-old cisgender female client is experiencing problems with anger. She yells at people who are driving near her, and she gets so upset at work that she leaves abruptly and without permission. She throws things at family members, but does not physically harm anyone.

She is usually very upset with herself, but reports having no control over her behavior.

Suggested Skills

- **Meta Skills:** This client can use the *Nonjudgmental* skill to suspend evaluations about herself and others, which will significantly diffuse the intensity of her emotions. *GIVE* will also be a useful skill for this client because it reminds her to be gentle and validating to others.

- **Secondary Skills:** *Half Smile* will help her find something in her day or in her life that she can have a genuine half smile about, which can help her feel a bit more relaxed. *4 Horsemen of the Apocalypse* will help her identify the four most destructive issues she brings into her relationships. She can then use mindfulness and other skills to keep these forces out of her relationships.

- **Ancillary Skill:** *Feeling Not Acting* will allow her to notice the emotion she is experiencing and to be present, which can allow her to identify her urges and choose to refrain from acting upon them. Instead, she can choose a skill to manage or tolerate impulses and urges.

List other skills with your reasoning/purpose for selecting them for the client, and how you would teach these skills to the client:

_____

_____

_____

_____

_____

_____

_____

ANXIETY DISORDERS

Clients diagnosed with an anxiety disorder may experience nervousness, worry, agitation and avoidance behavior that is specific to a situation or person (such as a phobia), or they can exhibit anxiety that is more generalized. This may also be accompanied by an inability to leave home and/or panic attacks due to irrational beliefs.

Dialectics

- Worrying a lot and wanting to be safe. Suggested skill: *Wise Mind*

- Hypersensitivity and being grounded in the body. Suggested skill: *Square Breathing*

- Worst-case scenario and having options. Suggested skill: *Keeping It In Perspective*

Mindfulness is very helpful for clients with anxiety because it helps them let go of any rumination about the past and any catastrophizing about the future. Mindfulness allows clients to be in the here-and-now with anxiety, pain and discomfort without thoughts such as, "It has always been this way," or "There is no hope of it changing in the future."

Distress Tolerance teaches these clients to tolerate their distress without exacerbating it. This takes active problem-solving some of the time and accepting reality at other times.

A tricky thing about anxiety is that when clients avoid the anxiety-provoking stimulus, it provides them temporary relief from the anxiety. This then reinforces avoidance as an effective strategy, even though avoidance is actually harmful in the long run. Continued avoidance results in decreased life satisfaction, impaired functioning, and damage to relationships. When a client is effective at tolerating their distress, they do not have to avoid life and can reduce the damage that avoidance causes.

Emotion Regulation helps clients manage their emotions on a daily basis, particularly those associated with anxiety. Clients learn about the connection among their emotions, energy levels, environmental cues and their anxiety.

Interpersonal Effectiveness helps clients continue to have healthy relationships even when experiencing anxiety.

Anxiety Disorders
Practice Vignette

A 27-year-old cisgender male is struggling with an inability to leave his house. He reports having panic attacks and worries that he is dying. He is fearful of being embarrassed or not being able to get out of a situation if there is a problem. This has been going on for about a year. Because of his anxiety, he has been getting in trouble at work and has a great deal of conflict in his marriage.

Suggested Skills

- **Meta Skills:** Using the *Nonjudgmental* skill can remind this client that he isn't "crazy," "damaged" or "sick" just because he has anxiety. The *DEAR SELF* skill can improve assertiveness and getting needs met in relationships by Describing what he wants, Encouraging others, Asking for what he needs, Reinforcing others, Sometimes tolerating not getting his way, Experiencing the present moment mindfully, Listening skillfully to himself and others and Finding negotiation opportunities.

- **Secondary Skills:** *Turtling* will encourage him to use a variety of skills to take care of himself. The *Self-Soothe Kit* can address all five of his senses—sight, sound, smell, taste and touch—and can be utilized when he is experiencing anxiety.

- **Ancillary Skill:** The *CARES* skill will help this client cope with anxiety by teaching him to remain Calm, monitor his Arousal, get Relaxation and rest, be mindful of Emotions in the environment and get a healthy amount of Sleep.

List other skills with your reasoning/purpose for selecting them for the client, and how you would teach these skills to the client:

_____

_____

_____

_____

_____

_____

_____

_____

_____

BIPOLAR DISORDER

Bipolar disorder involves mood swings ranging from mania or hypomania to depression. For some clients, these are rapid-cycling mood swings, while other clients only experience episodes every few months or years. When mania is at the extreme end, clients may be psychotic and engage in life-threatening behavior. Similarly, when depression is extreme, clients may have significant trouble taking care of their basic needs and may even be suicidal.

Medication is almost always included in the treatment protocol for clients with bipolar disorder. While medication can be very helpful, it often comes with side effects, and clients may dislike how they feel on the medication. Therefore, medication compliance tends to be a significant issue for clients with this diagnosis. Stopping the medication or not taking it as directed can lead to increased mood swings and negative life events.

Dialectics

- Wanting to have the mania while avoiding the depression. Suggested skill: *Ride the Wave*

- Having fun and taking care of oneself. Suggested skill: *MEDDSS*

- Energy and exhaustion. Suggested skill: *EMOTIONS*

Mindfulness is about staying in the present moment, which empowers these clients to move beyond previous mood swings and the destructive behaviors associated with them.

Distress Tolerance helps clients manage their crises and negative moods. When clients are able to manage frustrations more effectively, it helps them maintain a stable mood and can prevent an episode from being triggered.

Emotion Regulation encourages clients to track their emotions, engage in balanced self-care, and stay connected to their treatment professional. Emotion Regulation is particularly helpful for clients with bipolar disorder, as being sufficiently in tune with their emotions is necessary for them to notice when they may be gearing up or down emotionally. If that starts to happen, they can increase their self-care strategies and their use of DBT skills, as well as communicate with their psychiatric prescriber.

Interpersonal Effectiveness reminds clients with bipolar disorder to manage appropriate boundaries, maintain self-respect, and be assertive. By doing so, clients can establish and maintain stable relationships and healthy support systems, which also contribute to a stable mood.

Bipolar Disorder
Practice Vignette

A 37-year-old cisgender female reports a history of three previous manic episodes with accompanying hospitalizations. She also reports experiencing depression off and on throughout her life. A relapse of her depression seems to be indicated by her sleeping 10+ hours a night, calling in sick at work and withdrawing from her family. She also reports using methamphetamine and alcohol to avoid the depression and keep the mania going.

Suggested Skills

- **Meta Skills:** Perhaps the most important skill for bipolar clients is *MEDDSS*. This skill empowers the client to have a structured self-care regimen. Regular sleep hygiene, taking medication as prescribed, and not using illicit drugs are essential for establishing mood stability. With this skill, this client can do one or two things over which she has <u>M</u>astery; spend a few minutes <u>E</u>xercising, such as walking around the block or stretching; be thoughtful about her <u>D</u>iet; take prescription <u>D</u>rugs as directed and not use illicit drugs; get a healthy amount of <u>S</u>leep; and have a moment of <u>S</u>pirituality, connection or meaning. *Effectively* is also useful, since it encourages her to act in her best interest and focus on what works.

- **Secondary Skills:** The *Turtling* skill can encourage this client to use a variety of strategies to take care of herself. The *Broken Record* skill will encourage her to be a broken record with herself and to keep coming back to her needs even when dealing with her bipolar symptoms.

- **Ancillary Skill:** Using the *ONE MIND* skill can help her to stay grounded and in touch with her internal, environmental and interpersonal experiences. Doing <u>O</u>ne thing at a time, being in the here-and-<u>N</u>ow, being grounded in the <u>E</u>nvironment, staying in the <u>M</u>oment, <u>I</u>ncreasing her awareness of her five senses, being <u>N</u>onjudgmental with herself and others and <u>D</u>escribing what is going on can help her manage intense emotions or experiences in the moment.

List other skills with your reasoning/purpose for selecting them for the client, and how you would teach these skills to the client:

_____

_____

_____

_____

_____

CONDUCT DISORDER

Conduct disorder is a pattern of repetitive behavior where the rights of others or current social norms are violated. Symptoms include verbal and physical aggression, cruelty toward people and animals, destructive behavior, dishonesty, truancy, vandalism and stealing. When working with these individuals, it is important to connect with their self-interest and help them understand that acting pro-socially is in their best interest. Radically-Open DBT may be more effective for this diagnosis and symptoms than standard DBT.

Dialectics

- Self-interest and relationships with others. Suggested skill: *Relationship Assumptions*

- Feeling good and acting in one's best interests. Suggested skill: *Feeling Not Acting*

- Short-term goals and long-term plans. Suggested skill: *Ride the Wave*

Mindfulness can be particularly useful for clients with this diagnosis. Youth with conduct disorder are likely to ruminate about being disrespected or wronged, and they are also likely to plot future revenge for these slights. Mindfulness will help these clients stay in the here-and-now and let go of the past and future. It can also help move clients from assumptions about what is going on to actually being present with their experiences.

Distress Tolerance helps clients with conduct disorder by teaching them to manage their frustrations, so they do not destroy property, hurt others or hurt themselves.

Emotion Regulation can benefit clients greatly by having them get to know, and learn to manage, their emotions. These skills can help them learn to cope with emotions so they do not lose control and engage in problematic and destructive behaviors.

Interpersonal Effectiveness can be a critical area for clients with this diagnosis, since they can struggle with relationships—particularly with authority figures. Helping these clients invest in others while respecting themselves can dramatically reduce the incidence of problematic behavior. Interpersonal Effectiveness can also increase their confidence and competency.

Conduct Disorder
─── Practice Vignette ───

A 13-year-old cisgender male harms animals and attends school only 75% of the time. He often ignores the directions of his teachers and parents, and he gets upset with others and throws temper tantrums. He has gotten in trouble at school for seeking revenge against other children whom he believes did things to harm him.

Suggested Skills

- **Meta Skills:** *Effectively* can help this client be effective in his life by focusing on what is needed at a given moment, as opposed to what is the right or wrong choice, or what is fair or unfair. *Radical Acceptance* will help him let go of his controlling behaviors of others and the environment, and help him focus on what he does have control over: himself.

- **Secondary Skills:** The *Moment to Pause* skill can help this client interrupt his behavior to stop him from being destructive or acting out. In addition, the *Lemonade* skill will help him give himself credit for the strengths he has and his ability to survive difficulties.

- **Ancillary Skill:** *Turning the Mind* will remind him that he is in the driver's seat with his mind, not just a passenger in his life. This includes his thoughts, feelings, impulses and even behavior.

List other skills with your reasoning/purpose for selecting them for the client, and how you would teach these skills to the client:

_____

_____

_____

_____

_____

_____

_____

_____

_____

DEPRESSION

Depression can be intense and short-lived, or it can be more subtle and long-lasting. It may be accompanied by hopelessness and suicidal ideation, excessive or deficient eating and sleeping and an inability to have fun or enjoy usual activities.

Dialectics

- Hopelessness and optimism. Suggested skill: *Keeping It In Perspective*

- Pain and enjoyment. Suggested skill: *ACCEPTS*

- Past, present and future. Suggested skill: *ONE MIND*

Mindfulness is useful for clients with depression because it teaches them not to get stuck in the mindset that depression will last forever and never go away. Being in the here-and-now reduces rumination about how it has always been this way and that it will always be this way. Mindfulness also empowers clients to do what they can in the moment to take care of themselves.

Distress Tolerance provides clients with opportunities to effectively manage frustrations and stress, so the depression does not feel worse than it already is. Having increased Distress Tolerance also helps clients manage the hopelessness and suicidal feelings that may accompany their depression.

Emotion Regulation includes self-care strategies, but it also helps clients experience emotions other than depression, and develop strategies for changing their emotional experiences.

Interpersonal Effectiveness is important for clients with depression because it helps them continue to access their support system even when they feel they do not deserve to be cared about. These skills can combat the low self-esteem associated with mood disorders so that clients can be effective in their relationships.

Depression
—— Practice Vignette ——

A 21-year-old cisgender female reports that she sleeps 12–14 hours per day. She hasn't been eating much and has lost 20 pounds in the last two months. She also has very few friends, and she lost her job due to frequent absences and tardiness. Although she feels hopeless and wonders if life is worth living, she hasn't been suicidal in the past and there are no current concerns about lethal self-harm.

Suggested Skills

- **Meta Skills:** *FAST* can help this client be <u>F</u>air to herself, <u>A</u>pologize less, <u>S</u>tick to her values and be <u>T</u>ruthful with herself and others, which will increase her ability to manage her depression effectively. The self-care embedded in the *MEDDSS* skill is also useful for managing depression. This client can do one or two things she has <u>M</u>astered; spend a few minutes <u>E</u>xercising, such as walking around the block or stretching; be thoughtful about her <u>D</u>iet; take her prescription <u>D</u>rugs as directed and not use illicit drugs; get a healthy amount of <u>S</u>leep; and have a moment of <u>S</u>pirituality, connection or meaning.

- **Secondary Skills:** *Crisis Survival Network* can help this client feel supported and manage stress by having a list of people who support her and help her deal with difficulties. *Relationship Mindfulness* will help this client identify generalizations, describe assumptions, suspend judgments, avoid jumping to conclusions, be self-empowering and not self-defeating and be nonjudgmental in her relationships.

- **Ancillary Skill:** *Observe, Describe & Participate* will help her just notice and become aware of things in this one moment. She can describe experiences in concrete, specific, nonjudgmental terms and engage fully and completely in each activity—particularly self-care.

List other skills with your reasoning/purpose for selecting them for the client, and how you would teach these skills to the client:

_____

_____

_____

_____

_____

EATING DISORDERS

Eating disorders can include restricting food intake, binging/purging or overeating. They can be accompanied by unrealistic body image and feelings of being out of control.

Dialectics

- Indulgence and restraint. Suggested skill: *IMPROVE*

- Control and ability to let go. Suggested skill: *Repairs*

- Enjoyment and deprivation. Suggested skill: *Wise Mind*

Mindfulness is essential for these clients, since it will help them stay present with the ritual of eating while being nonjudgmental.

Distress Tolerance assists clients in managing crises and internal distress without having to resort to restricting or binging.

Emotion Regulation provides clients with the tools to manage emotions and impulses by engaging in healthy self-care. When clients manage their emotions more effectively, it may help reduce their urges to engage in disordered eating.

Interpersonal Effectiveness helps clients establish healthy boundaries, effective communication and self-respect.

Eating Disorders
── Practice Vignette ──

A 14-year-old cisgender female oscillates between restrictive eating and binging and purging behavior. She has an unrealistic body image, and she is slightly underweight but not significantly. Additionally, her family is highly conflictual. She excels academically but doesn't have any close friends, and she doesn't get involved in after-school or recreational activities.

Suggested Skills

- **Meta Skills:** *Radical Acceptance* will help this client and her support system to understand that she can influence and impact others but not control them. The only thing individuals have control over is themselves, and therefore she can focus on her behaviors, thoughts and emotions. When she finds ways to feel in control, she can disengage from her problematic eating behavior. In addition, *FAST* will help her be <u>F</u>air to herself, <u>A</u>pologize less, <u>S</u>tick to her values and be <u>T</u>ruthful with herself and others, which can increase her ability to manage her eating and compensatory behaviors effectively.

- **Secondary Skills:** The *Self-Soothe Kit* will encourage this client to create a kit that is self-soothing and use it when needed. The kit can be used before, during and after eating. Nothing in the box can be destructive—such as laxatives—even though the client may describe them as soothing. *Turtling* can teach her to use a variety of strategies to take care of herself, not just the ones she is using with food.

- **Ancillary Skill:** The *BEHAVIOR* skill will encourage this client to use effective <u>B</u>ehavior, be grounded in the <u>E</u>nvironment, do things that are <u>H</u>ealing not hurting, <u>A</u>ct in her best interest, be consistent with her <u>V</u>alues, <u>I</u>magine getting through difficulties, focus on her desired <u>O</u>utcome and <u>R</u>einforce her successes.

List other skills with your reasoning/purpose for selecting them for the client, and how you would teach these skills to the client:

_____

_____

_____

_____

_____

_____

GRIEF AND LOSS

Grief and loss can occur in response to a death or other interpersonal loss, accidents or trauma. As clients navigate their grief, they may experience depression, anxiety and a variety of strong emotions, among other symptoms.

Dialectics

- Grieving the loss while appreciating one's life. Suggested skill: *Keeping It In Perspective*

- Letting the grief run its course while not making it any worse than it already is. Suggested skill: *EMOTIONS*

- Making peace with really painful situations. Suggested skill: *Willingness*

Mindfulness is useful for clients dealing with grief and loss because it helps them be intentional about remembering the past and planning for the future, while being in the here-and-now most of the time. Mindfulness also helps clients avoid any guilt or shame by being nonjudgmental and effective.

Distress Tolerance can be essential for clients dealing with grief and loss by reminding them to balance active problem-solving strategies with a willingness to accept the situation when it cannot be changed. If there are feelings of hopelessness or despair, Distress Tolerance can help clients be as effective as possible.

Emotion Regulation is another area that is very useful for grief and loss. It encourages on-going self-care even when clients have strong emotions and little energy. It also helps fight thoughts of "Why bother?" or "It doesn't matter anyway."

Interpersonal Effectiveness can provide comfort and support for those dealing with grief and loss by facilitating healthy relationships.

Grief and Loss
Practice Vignette

The client is a 37-year-old cisgender male, an outspoken advocate for the gay community, who recently lost his partner of 16 years to AIDs. Fortunately, he is HIV negative. He has lost a number of other friends to the virus over the last 20 years. He reports being enormously sad, has little appetite, is not sleeping and wishes he wasn't in so much pain. He appears to have a functional support system who check on him regularly to make sure he eats and gets out of his apartment. He is working a reduced schedule at work for the next three months—although the only time he stops thinking about his partner's death is when he is at work.

Suggested Skills

- **Meta Skills:** *Radical Acceptance* will help this client accept what is out of his control. In the case of grief, clients can learn to accept the loss and emotions that accompany it, while focusing on what they do have control over: themselves. Radical acceptance does not mean that this client approves of his losses or believes that they are ok, but he can accept that this is his reality and that he needs to work with it. Additionally, the *DEAR SELF* skill will teach this client that he can deal with his grief by Describing what he wants, Encouraging others to help, Asking for what he wants, Reinforcing others to help him, Sometimes tolerating not getting his way, Experiencing the present moment mindfully, Listening skillfully to himself and others and Finding negotiation opportunities.

- **Secondary Skills:** *Be Mindful* is useful for this client because it can remind him to be aware of the importance of self-care and to use his skills. *Crisis Survival Network* will help this client reduce isolation and receive support from his support system, with an emphasis on not over-relying on one person. He can use his *Crisis Survival Network* to distract himself in healthy ways.

- **Ancillary Skill:** The *BEHAVIOR* skill can teach this client to use effective Behavior, be grounded in the Environment, do things that are Healing not hurting, Act in his best interest, be consistent with his Values, Imagine getting through his difficulties, focus on his desired Outcome and Reinforce his successes.

List other skills with your reasoning/purpose for selecting them for the client, and how you would teach these skills to the client:

_____

_____

_____

IMPULSE CONTROL PROBLEMS

Both youth and adults may find it hard to maintain self-control. Sometimes impulsivity is when individuals act quickly without thinking through their choices or behaviors. Other times it is not rapid, but the scale of the choices or behavior is large, such as quitting a job or dropping out of school.

Dialectics

- Right now and in a little while. Suggested skill: *Feeling Not Acting*

- Willfulness and self-discipline. Suggested skill: *Willingness*

- Yes and no. Suggested skill: *DEAR SELF*

Mindfulness is about slowing down and staying in the moment, which helps these clients learn to be with their impulses without necessarily acting on them.

Distress Tolerance helps clients learn to be less impulsive by giving them something to do besides acting on an impulse—such as a replacement behavior or a healthy distraction.

Emotion Regulation helps clients manage emotions effectively and can reduce or eliminate impulsivity.

Interpersonal Effectiveness is about being heard and validated in relationships along with the ability to agree to disagree, which are both likely to reduce impulsivity. Wanting to be effective in relationships can provide motivation to improve the management of impulses.

Impulse Control Problems
Practice Vignette

A 16-year-old cisgender male can't seem to control himself. He drinks his parents' alcohol, plays video games for hours and gets upset at school—yelling and using obscenities. He has had one occasion of harming the family pet, and he is suspected of graffiti in the neighborhood.

Suggested Skills

- **Meta Skills:** *Wise Mind* will encourage this client to balance Rational Mind and Emotional Mind to create Wise Mind. When in Wise Mind, this client can make better decisions and be intentional about his behavior. *GIVE* can also help him be aware of the impact his behavior has on others, and can encourage him to invest in relationships. He can be <u>G</u>entle in relationships, show <u>I</u>nterest in others, <u>V</u>alidate others and have an <u>E</u>asy manner.

- **Secondary Skills:** *Ride the Wave* can be a crucial skill for managing impulses. Our emotions and impulses are just like the tides that come and go, and they are always with us. Some days are stormy and chaotic, while other days are calmer. This client can imagine that he is riding the wave of his impulses by envisioning surfing, snowboarding, skiing or skateboarding. In addition, *Lemonade* will encourage this client to work to his strengths and redirect his energy to more prosocial endeavors. Instead of drawing graffiti in his neighborhood, he can create art. Using the *Moment to Pause* skill will also help him have more control.

- **Ancillary Skill:** *Willingness* exercises will be helpful in the middle of a crisis or when this client is feeling impulsive. He can practice willingness to accept reality, a bad day, things not going his way or the fact that he can't control others and the world around him.

List other skills with your reasoning/purpose for selecting them for the client, and how you would teach these skills to the client:

_____

_____

_____

_____

_____

_____

INADEQUATE STRESS MANAGEMENT

Stress management is a basic competency most individuals can benefit from, regardless of whether or not they meet diagnostic criteria for a mental health disorder. Unfortunately, many clients don't have sufficient stress management skills to cope effectively with their chaotic and out-of-control lives.

Dialectics

- Having stress and finding ways to relax. Suggested skill: *Self-Soothe Kit*

- Experiencing difficulties and figuring out how to deal with them. Suggested skill: *Observe, Describe & Participate*

- Not always knowing what to do while not making it worse than it already is. Suggested skill: *Effectively*

Mindfulness is a useful tool for stress management, as it helps clients stop ruminating about the past and catastrophizing about the future. Instead, clients learn to focus on the present moment and manage their stress and problems effectively.

Distress Tolerance is also an important aspect of effective stress management. Distress Tolerance techniques teach clients how to actively problem-solve the situations they have control over, while also being willing to accept the realities that are out of their control.

Emotion Regulation reduces clients' overall stress by teaching them how to cope with emotions on a daily basis in an effective manner.

Interpersonal Effectiveness helps clients manage stress and difficulties more effectively by tapping into their support systems.

Inadequate Stress Management
Practice Vignette

A 27-year-old transgender male, who worked at an investment firm that went bankrupt last month, comes into therapy. He is very stressed about his finances and what he will do about work. He reports that he wants to change careers so he doesn't have to deal with people losing everything; however, he has no idea what else he wants to do. Fortunately, he has enough money to pay his bills for four months, but he loses sleep about what he is going to do after that. His family is supportive, and he has a girlfriend who wants him to take some time for himself.

Suggested Skills

- **Meta Skills:** *MEDDSS* is a skill that can be practiced on a daily basis to help this client deal with stress more effectively. With this skill, he can do one or two things over which he has <u>M</u>astery; spend a few minutes <u>E</u>xercising, such as walking around the block or stretching; be thoughtful about his <u>D</u>iet; take prescription <u>D</u>rugs as directed and not use illicit drugs; get a healthy amount of <u>S</u>leep; and have a moment of <u>S</u>pirituality, connection or meaning. Additionally, using *Wise Mind* can help him make choices to reduce stress and remember the things that are going well in his life.

- **Secondary Skills:** Using the *Half Smile* skill will help him to find positives in his life amidst the overwhelming stress. Perhaps he can also use the *Lemonade* skill by redirecting his job skills to help individuals and his community.

- **Ancillary Skill:** This client can *Turn the Tables* to contribute and make relationships and the community better—which, in turn, may improve his perspective when he realizes that he can make a difference.

List other skills with your reasoning/purpose for selecting them for the client, and how you would teach these skills to the client:

_____

_____

_____

_____

_____

_____

LOW SELF-ESTEEM

Individuals with low self-esteem lack confidence and have negative feelings about themselves. There may be significant amounts of shame, guilt and other negative self-judgments. While low self-esteem is not a formal mental health diagnosis, many clients dealing with mental health concerns display low self-esteem.

Dialectics

- Not believing in oneself while believing that one has things to contribute in relationships. Suggested skill: *Broken Record*

- Being imperfect while striving to improve. Suggested skill: *Love Dandelions*

- Feeling like a failure while acknowledging strengths. Suggested skill: *SPECIFIC PATHS*

Mindfulness is useful for this client concern because it helps them learn to let go of perceived past failures and to stop worrying about being "less than" in the future. Mindfulness provides individuals with the opportunity to improve and grow in the here-and-now.

Distress Tolerance is helpful for these clients because it provides them with the tools to deal with stress, which can lead to increased competencies and confidence in their abilities.

Emotion Regulation can increase these clients' self-esteem by teaching them to manage their impulses and feelings effectively.

Interpersonal Effectiveness demonstrates to clients with low self-esteem that they can have healthy, functional relationships while also maintaining their own identities.

Low Self-Esteem
──── Practice Vignette ────

A 23-year-old cisgender male calls to get into therapy. Although he has a degree in computer science, he's working a minimum-wage job pumping gas. He says he feels worthless, he has nothing to offer his girlfriend and he doesn't know why she stays with him. He enjoys creating graphic novels, but doesn't do it often because he thinks his stories are "stupid." Instead, he reports that his weekends are spent sitting on the couch staring at the TV. He says most of his friends are losers just like him. In college, everyone thought he had a bright future ahead of him, but none of that has come true.

Suggested Skills

- **Meta Skills:** *Nonjudgmental* will remind this client that he has weaknesses and is dealing with challenges, but that doesn't make him a failure or unlovable. *FAST* will teach him to value himself and be assertive by being <u>F</u>air to himself, <u>A</u>pologizing less, <u>S</u>ticking to his values and being <u>T</u>ruthful with himself.

- **Secondary Skills:** Even when he feels bad about himself or faces setbacks, he can find something in his life to have a *Half Smile* about, which will help him relax and will improve his mood. Given that clients with low self-esteem may also focus on their weaknesses, the *Lemonade* skill is useful to this client because it helps him turn perceived weaknesses into strengths.

- **Ancillary Skill:** It is beneficial for this client to learn how to *Observe, Describe & Participate* in his life nonjudgmentally. Being able to participate is particularly useful in encouraging him to fully invest in and live his life even when he does not believe he deserves to.

List other skills with your reasoning/purpose for selecting them for the client, and how you would teach these skills to the client:

_____

_____

_____

_____

_____

_____

_____

OPPOSITIONAL DEFIANT DISORDER

Oppositional defiant disorder entails an ongoing pattern of disobedient, hostile and defiant behavior toward authority figures that goes beyond the bounds of normal childhood behavior. It may also represent the beginning of an ongoing path of difficulties in this area, as it may lead to the development of conduct disorder and antisocial personality disorder. Radically-Open DBT may be more effective than standard DBT for this diagnosis and set of symptoms.

Dialectics

- Having fun without engaging in delinquent behavior. Suggested skill: *Turning the Mind*

- Disliking school while continuing to participate in the educational process. Suggested skill: *Feeling Not Acting*

- Enjoying being a kid while maturing into a young adult. Suggested skill: *Keeping It In Perspective*

Mindfulness helps clients with oppositional defiant disorder stay in the here-and-now and not get caught up in planning future revenge or thinking about previous disappointments.

Distress Tolerance also provides these clients with the tools to manage frustrations and difficulties so they can avoid acting out.

Emotion Regulation provides these clients with competencies that are essential for day-to-day management of emotions and impulses. By using Emotion Regulation strategies, these clients can learn how to better control their impulses, which can help deter acting-out behaviors.

Interpersonal Effectiveness gives these clients the opportunity to build healthy relationships based on respect, mutuality and integrity.

Oppositional Defiant Disorder
Practice Vignette

A 15-year-old cisgender female is brought in by her older sister, whom she lives with. Her parents kicked her out because they were ashamed of her behavior. She is failing several subjects in school, she plays video games for hours even when she has homework and chores to do and her parents discovered that she had sent and received over 10,000 text messages last month. In addition to this, she has been caught on sexually-explicit websites. She seems to do whatever she wants regardless of the rules or expectations of others.

Suggested Skills

- **Meta Skills:** *Effectively* will help this client be effective in her life by focusing on what is needed at a given moment, as opposed to what she thinks is the right or wrong choice, or what is fair or unfair. *Wise Mind* can help her be thoughtful and reflective to manage her emotionality.

- **Secondary Skills:** This client can learn prosocial attitudes and behaviors from the *Teenage Mutant Ninja Turtles* and then practice *Turtling* at school, at home and when interacting with others. *Turtling* will teach her to use a variety of strategies to take care of herself just like turtles do. In addition, the *Moment to Pause* skill will help her interrupt her behavior to stop being destructive or acting out.

- **Ancillary Skill:** *Dealing with Difficult People* is another useful skill for this client because it will help her to understand her relationships better and to focus on improving what she has control over.

List other skills with your reasoning/purpose for selecting them for the client, and how you would teach these skills to the client:

_____

_____

_____

_____

_____

_____

_____

RELATIONAL PROBLEMS

Although relationship difficulties can occur in familial relationships and friendships, the focus of this section is on intimate relationships such as marriages or domestic partnerships. Individuals with intimate relationship difficulties may exhibit a high level of conflict, dishonesty, problematic communication styles or impaired boundaries.

Dialectics

- Caring about one another and being annoyed or frustrated with the other person. Suggested skill: *Relationship Mindfulness*

- Taking care of oneself while investing in the other person. Suggested skill: *Turning the Tables*

- Being able to appreciate things from multiple perspectives. Suggested skill: *Relationship Assumptions*

Mindfulness helps clients experiencing relational difficulties let go of long-standing conflicts and focus on what works in the relationship, instead of being right or winning disagreements.

Distress Tolerance gives these clients tools to deal with conflict and stress in an effective way, which also provides them with an opportunity to invest in the relationship.

Emotion Regulation helps couples manage their emotions and impulses to more effectively reduce distress.

Interpersonal Effectiveness will help the couple reduce judgments, encourage collaboration, and focus on solutions, which will increase their relational effectiveness.

Relational Problems
Practice Vignette

A heterosexual couple married for 48 years comes in for therapy. The husband recently retired, and the wife retired two years ago. Lately they have been having a lot of conflicts because they are spending so much time together. Their adult children and grandchildren live on the other side of the country, and they only have a few friends. Furthermore, neither of them seem to have many hobbies, and they both report not knowing what to do with their time and don't seem to have a sense of purpose now that they aren't working. They do attend church on a regular basis. After so many years of marriage, they can't believe that they are having these problems. Neither has been in therapy before.

Suggested Skills

- **Meta Skills:** It is important for each member of the relationship to use *GIVE* and *FAST*, which focus on increasing the ability to build a healthy relationship while maintaining self-respect. *GIVE* reminds couples to be <u>G</u>entle with one another, be <u>I</u>nterested in one another, <u>V</u>alidate the other person's perspective and to have an <u>E</u>asy manner. *FAST* reinforces the importance of also being <u>F</u>air to oneself, <u>A</u>pologizing less, <u>S</u>ticking to one's values and being <u>T</u>ruthful with oneself and others.

- **Secondary Skills:** *Repairs* will help each of them make apologies, accept apologies and let some things go. Additionally, they will benefit from *4 Horsemen of the Apocalypse* by identifying each of the four horsemen they bring into their relationship and then figuring out how to reduce or eliminate each of these horsemen.

- **Ancillary Skill:** The *ABC* skill is also helpful in teaching clients with relational difficulties to <u>A</u>ccumulate positives, <u>B</u>uild mastery and <u>C</u>ope ahead for the health of the relationship.

List other skills with your reasoning/purpose for selecting them for the client, and how you would teach these skills to the client:

_____

_____

_____

_____

_____

_____

SUBSTANCE USE DISORDER: MILD

Substance use disorders include a range of problems related to the use of alcohol and other drugs. In addition, these disorders are thought to have a biopsychosocial etiology. Individuals with a substance use disorder tend to relapse on a chronic basis and may require ongoing or multiple episodes of treatment.

Dialectics

- Having fun without using substances. Suggested skill: *Wise Mind*

- Ability to effectively manage stress without making it worse through the use of substances. Suggested skill: *Nonjudgmental*

- Making significant changes in one's life while remaining true to oneself. Suggested skill: *SPECIFIC PATHS*

Mindfulness is particularly useful for individuals with a substance use disorder, as it teaches them that life can be lived as "one day at a time." Helping these clients focus on what they need to work on today, and what they need to do to get through the day without using substances, is essential. Staying in the moment can help clients focus on the tasks at hand and reduce avoidance behaviors that lead to the use of substances.

Distress Tolerance enables these clients to more effectively manage stress and difficulties, which empowers them to focus on their recoveries and avoid reengaging their addictions.

Emotion Regulation skills provide these clients with the tools necessary to manage their emotions and impulses effectively, which increases stability and life satisfaction.

Interpersonal Effectiveness helps these clients repair existing relationships and build new, healthy relationships. By being more functional in their relationships, clients may find less need for substances.

Substance Use Disorder: Mild
Practice Vignette

A 24-year-old cisgender female uses marijuana and alcohol a couple of times a week. She has missed work a couple of times in the last year. Although she has a job at which she seems to do well and her home life is stable, she reports wanting more from life. She says she plans to go back to school but doesn't seem to get around to it. Additionally, her self-care seems impaired; she sleeps a lot and eats more than she wants to.

Suggested Skills

- **Meta Skills:** Learning to be *Nonjudgmental* with both herself and others can help this client disengage from her addictive behavior, since the negative judgments that she is making about herself fosters her continued substance use. In addition, *Effectively* will help her learn how to manage her stress and engage in healthy relationships so that she doesn't need substances as much.

- **Secondary Skills:** This client can *Be Mindful* of using skills, engaging in self-care, having healthy fun, and connecting with a support system, which can help reduce her reliance on substances to feel like she can function. Given the damage that addiction does to relationships, she will also benefit from making effective *Repairs* to provide building blocks for new, healthy relationships.

- **Ancillary Skill:** The *IMPROVE* skill will encourage this client to distract herself with Imagery of a beautiful or safe place, find Meaning in her life, engage in Prayer, Relax, do One thing at a time, take a Vacation from the demands of her life and use Encouragement to be effective.

List other skills with your reasoning/purpose for selecting them for the client, and how you would teach these skills to the client:

_____

_____

_____

_____

_____

_____

_____

SUBSTANCE USE DISORDER: SEVERE

Severe substance use is often characterized by a loss of control, cravings, tolerance to the substance and withdrawal. The individual may have made several attempts to cut down or stop use, but these have often been unsuccessful.

Dialectics

- Denying reality and knowing the truth about their addiction. Suggested skill: *BEHAVIOR*

- Deceiving self and others about their addiction and associated behavior. Suggested skill: *Turtling*

- Persistence and giving up trying to be healthy. Suggested skill: *Feeling Not Acting*

Mindfulness can be quite empowering and essential to establishing recovery. It helps clients struggling with addiction to be present in the here-and-now, because they may spend very little time in the present during their addiction.

Distress Tolerance can also be extremely useful to these clients, since they may have very little tolerance for frustration or pain.

Emotion Regulation helps these clients effectively manage the intensity of their emotions, urges and impulsive behaviors—which can be overpowering and prompt relapses.

Interpersonal Effectiveness helps these clients increase their effectiveness in relationships. Because their relationships may be impaired due to their addictions, they can benefit greatly from being more skillful and effective in this area.

Substance Use Disorder: Severe
—— Practice Vignette ——

A 56-year-old cisgender male has been using alcohol, marijuana and cocaine for most of his adult life. Although he has been through treatment before, he has only been able to maintain sobriety for a few months. He uses because it is "fun" and helps him feel "normal;" he reports having cravings that he manages by using.

Suggested Skills

- **Meta Skills:** Because clients with addiction issues often engage in very little or no self-care, *MEDDSS* will help this client start taking care of himself by focusing on <u>M</u>astery, <u>E</u>xercise, <u>D</u>iet, <u>D</u>rugs (prescribed medications), <u>S</u>leep and <u>S</u>pirituality. In addition, *Radical Acceptance* can help him focus on what he has control over: his own thoughts, feelings, impulses and behaviors. This skill will also help him let go of what he can't control: others, and the world around him.

- **Secondary Skills:** *Moment to Pause* can help this client to take a quick moment to check in with himself, his environment and his interactions. *Crisis Survival Network* is also an important tool that will provide this client with the support and encouragement he needs to stay off drugs and alcohol. Instead of resorting to drugs or alcohol, he can turn to individuals from his network in a time of need.

- **Ancillary Skill:** *EMOTIONS* is another important skill that will teach this client to <u>E</u>xpose himself to his emotions, be <u>M</u>indful of his current emotions, <u>O</u>utline a plan to deal with his emotions, <u>T</u>ake opposite action, <u>I</u>ncrease his positive experiences, identify <u>O</u>bstacles and develop plans to overcome them, <u>N</u>otice what is going on and access his <u>S</u>upport system.

List other skills with your reasoning/purpose for selecting them for the client, and how you would teach these skills to the client:

_____

_____

_____

_____

_____

_____

TRAUMA (SINGLE)

Clients can develop traumatic reactions in response to having been threatened, abused or violated in childhood or adulthood. Furthermore, experiencing poverty, oppression and even disasters can all result in trauma reactions. Clients may experience multiple traumas, a single trauma or chronic traumatic situations. However, each person's response to their experiences is unique. For instance, individuals may experience the same or similar situations; one person may be traumatized, while another may become resilient.

Dialectics

- Disempowered and empowered. Suggested skill: *Half Smile*

- Victim and survivor. Suggested skill: *Lemonade*

- Danger and safety. Suggested skill: *DEAR SELF*

Mindfulness helps these clients stop reliving the traumatic event by keeping them in the here-and-now. This present-moment awareness also helps them recognize that the events are not happening in the current moment despite physiological and emotional cues that may suggest otherwise, allowing them to ground themselves and reduce their arousal.

Distress Tolerance helps to reduce hypervigilance. In addition, it helps these clients manage their crises by providing them with the tools to handle frustrations and difficulties so they can use healthy distractions.

Emotion Regulation can be used to manage the emotional intensity associated with trauma, because it provides the competencies essential for day-to-day management of emotions and impulses. By using Emotion Regulation, clients can instill impulse control.

Interpersonal Effectiveness can help clients have appropriate assertiveness, self-respect and investment in relationships.

Trauma (Single)
Practice Vignette

A 17-year-old transgender female was sexually abused by a next-door neighbor when she was 11 years old. She thinks a lot about the event and is having trouble sleeping, is easily startled and cries a lot. Although she knows she is missing out on many typical teenage activities, she can't trust other people.

Suggested Skills

- **Meta Skills:** This client can use the *FAST* skills to help establish boundaries and a sense of self. She can be <u>F</u>air to herself, <u>A</u>pologize less, <u>S</u>tick to her values and be <u>T</u>ruthful with herself. She can also use the *Wise Mind* skill to find balance with thinking and feeling.

- **Secondary Skills:** By using the *Turtling* skill, she can take care of herself like a turtle. She can retreat inside herself for safety sometimes, go slowly and methodically, protect herself but not be aggressive, be adaptive in a variety of situations, use her hard outer shell to let others' judgments roll off her back and persistently get herself back in balance.

- **Ancillary Skill:** The *CARES* skill will empower this client to manage her emotions by being <u>C</u>alm, monitoring <u>A</u>rousal, finding <u>R</u>elaxation and rest, coping with her <u>E</u>motions and getting a healthy amount of <u>S</u>leep.

List other skills with your reasoning/purpose for selecting them for the client, and how you would teach these skills to the client:

_____

_____

_____

_____

_____

_____

_____

_____

TRAUMA (COMPLEX)

Far too many people experience complex or multiple traumas. This can be ongoing physical, psychological and sexual abuse. It can also include dealing with major medical problems that require multiple invasive procedures, or intergenerational trauma caused by oppression and racism.

Dialectics:

- Living life fully even when danger is possible. Suggested skill: *Observe, Describe & Participate*

- Finding ways to be safe in an unsafe and chaotic world. Suggested skill: *Radical Acceptance*

- Investing in safe relationships while taking care of self. Suggested skill: *Relationship Assumptions*

Mindfulness helps these clients be grounded in the present moment, while still being connected to the trauma. It also encourages them to take care of themselves and be safe on a daily basis.

Distress Tolerance is essential for managing the aftermath of trauma while also managing daily stressors in an effective manner.

Emotion Regulation encourages clients to manage emotions and impulses to support stability and safety.

Interpersonal Effectiveness is about building relationship skills to ensure safety and interpersonal connection and support.

Trauma (Complex)
—— Practice Vignette ——

The client is a 49-year-old Native American cisgender male who was raised on a reservation in poverty. There is a history of intergenerational trauma in his family and tribe. He moved off the reservation to go to college and has not been back. Currently, he works two low-paying jobs to make ends meet. He has a history of being taken advantage of by women, and his most recent stressor was being mugged on his way home from work after midnight. He is having trouble sleeping, feels unsafe, believes people are following him, startles easily and feels empty on the inside.

Suggested Skills

- **Meta Skills:** *Effectively* will empower this client to be safe while also living his life. *MEDDSS* can help him remember to take care of himself, while reducing exhaustion and hypervigilance through <u>M</u>astery, <u>E</u>xercise, <u>D</u>iet, <u>D</u>rugs (prescribed medications), <u>S</u>leep and <u>S</u>pirituality.

- **Secondary Skills:** *Self-Soothe Kit* will help this client soothe himself in safe ways that will help him stay grounded. In addition, *Crisis Survival Network* will empower him to stay in touch with, and connect with, healthy supports.

- **Ancillary Skill:** This client can manage his emotions by using *CARES* to be <u>C</u>alm, monitor his <u>A</u>rousal, get <u>R</u>elaxation and rest, be mindful of his <u>E</u>motions in different environments, and get a healthy amount of <u>S</u>leep.

List other skills with your reasoning/purpose for selecting them for the client, and how you would teach these skills to the client:

_____

_____

_____

_____

_____

_____

_____

References

For your convenience, purchasers of this book can download and print worksheets and handouts from www.pesi.com/DBTGUIDE

Baer, R. A. (2014). *Mindfulness-Based Treatment Approaches: Clinician's Guide to Evidence Base and Applications* (2nd ed.). Cambridge, MA: Academic Press.

Bowen, S., Chawla, N., and Martlatt, G. A. (2010). *Mindfulness-Based Relapse Prevention for Addictive Behaviors: A Clinician's Guide.* New York, NY: Guilford Press.

Erikson, E. and Erikson, J. (1997). *The Life Cycle Completed.* New York, NY: Norton & Co.

Hayes, S. C., Stroshal, K. D., and Wilson, K. G. (2016). *Acceptance and Commitment Therapy: The Process and Practice of Mindful Change* (2nd ed.). New York, NY: Guilford Press.

Linehan, M. (1993a). *Cognitive-Behavioral Treatment of Borderline Personality Disorder.* New York, NY: Guilford Press.

Linehan, M. (1993b). *Skills Training Manual for Treating Borderline Personality Disorder.* New York, NY: Guilford Press.

Linehan, M. (2015). *DBT Skills Training Manual* (2nd ed.). New York, NY: Guilford Press.

Lynch, T. R. (2018). *Radically Open Dialectical Behavior Therapy: Theory and Practice for Treating Disorders of Over Control.* Oakland, CA: Context Press.

Max-Neef, M. A. (1989). *Human Scale Development: Conception, Application and Further Reflections.* New York, NY: Apex Press.

Miller, W. R. and Rollnick, S. (2012). *Motivational Interviewing: Helping People Change* (3rd ed.). New York, NY: Guilford Press.

Prochaska, J. O., Norcross, J., and DiClemente, C. (1994). *Changing for Good: A Revolutionary Six-Stage Program for Overcoming Bad Habits and Moving Your Life Positively Forward.* Fort Mill, SC: Quill House Publishers.

Prochaska, J. O. and Prochaska, J. M. (2016). *Changing to Thrive: Using the Stages of Change to Overcome the Top Threats to Your Health and Happiness.* Center City, MN: Hazelton Publishing.

Swales, M. A. and Heard, H. L. (2016). *Dialectical Behaviour Therapy: Distinctive Features* (2nd ed.). New York, NY: Routledge Publishers.

Made in the USA
San Bernardino, CA
12 February 2020